CLOISTER

BOOKS

Cloister Books are inspired by the monastic custom of walking slowly and reading or meditating in the monastery cloister, a place of silence, centering, and calm. Within these pages you will find a similar space in which to pray and reflect on the presence of God.

My Soul in Silence Waits

My Soul in Silence Waits

MEDITATIONS ON PSALM 62

Margaret Guenther

COWLEY PUBLICATIONS
Cambridge • Boston
Massachusetts

Published in the United States of America by Cowley Publications, a division of the Society of St. John the Evangelist. No portion of this book may be reproduced, stored in or introduced into a retrieval system, or transmitted, in any form or by any means—including photocopying—without the prior written permission of Cowley Publications, except in the case of brief quotations embedded in critical articles and reviews.

Library of Congress Cataloging-in-Publication Data:
Guenther, Margaret, 1930–

    My soul in silence waits: reflections on Psalm 62 / Margaret Guenther.

    p. cm.

    Includes bibliographical references.

    ISBN 1-56101-181-9

    1. Retreats. 2. Bible. O.T. Psalms LXII—Criticism, interpretation, etc. I. Title.

BV5068.R4 G84 2000

269'.6—dc21   00-043191

Scripture quotations are taken from *The New Revised Standard Version* of the Bible, © 1989, by the Division of Christian Education of the National Council of the Churches of Christ in the United States of America. Used by permission. Quotations from the Psalms are taken from the 1979 *Book of Common Prayer.*

Cynthia Shattuck, editor; Annie Kammerer, copyeditor; Vicki Black, designer. Cover photograph: *"Golden Daisy, Bugaboo Glacier Provincial Park"* by Dave Schiefelbein.

This book was printed on recycled acid-free paper by Versa Press in the United States of America.

Cowley Publications
28 Temple Place • Boston, Massachusetts 02111
800-225-1534 • www.cowley.org

For Elizabeth, Katherine, and John

Contents

Acknowledgments

I wish to express my gratitude to Cowley Publications for a collegial working relationship that has been fruitful and stimulating. It has been a special pleasure to work with Vicki Black and Annie Kammerer. To Cynthia Shattuck—friend, critic, and fellow movie buff—I can only say, "Thank you!"

We do not know who wrote the psalms, the songs and prayers of a whole people. Solely for convenience, I have referred to the author(s) as the psalmist.

As always, I am deeply grateful to my husband Jack for his support in the writing of this book.

Come Away
and Rest

The apostles gathered around Jesus, and told him all they had done and taught. He said to them, "Come away to a deserted place all by yourselves and rest a while." For many were coming and going, and they had no leisure even to eat. (Mark 6:30-31)

This was no ordinary busy time for Jesus and his friends. He had sent out the twelve to teach and heal, and he himself was going among the villages teaching. What's more, there had been a disastrous visit to his hometown. *Who does this upstart think he is?* was the reaction of the folk who had known him all his life, "and they took offense at him" (Mark 6:3). Most ominous for his ministry, though, was news of the fate of John the Baptizer, beheaded by Herod in prison. All in all, it was not a good time to turn his back on harsh reality and seek rest. Flight perhaps might be prudent, but not prayerful withdrawal for replenishment and re-creation.

In our hyperactive, high-achieving society, it is good to hold this picture of Jesus before us. He knew when it was time to retreat, seek a new spiritual landscape, and correct his perspective. This was not an isolated incident: again and again, Jesus removed himself from the scene of action. Periodically, he stopped preaching, teaching, healing, arguing with those authorities who wanted to trip him up. He left behind the people who wanted to share a meal with him, and those who just wanted a glimpse of him, or a chance to touch the hem of his garment. Most of us are tightly scheduled, burdened with obligations ranging from the sublime to the ridiculous, so that the very idea of walking away, simply withdrawing for a little while from the demands of the alleged "real" world, seems absurd if not impossible—even if we do not live in fear of Herod's executioner or the withering scorn of our neighbors. Jesus shows us a rhythm of going out and coming back, of departure and return almost like the regular, life-sustaining rhythm of respiration.

Mark gives us an especially vivid picture of Jesus' seeming dereliction of duty:

> That evening, at sundown, they brought to him all who were sick or possessed with demons. And the whole city was gathered around the door. And he cured many who were sick with various diseases, and cast out many demons. . . . In the morning, while it was still very dark, he got up and went out to a deserted place, and there he prayed. (Mark 1:32-35)

Peter and the disciples have to hunt him down to tell him that everyone is looking for him. Jesus responds, "Let us go on to the neighboring towns" (Mark 1:38). As one with a compulsion to get the job done, indeed, to be a model of efficiency leaving no loose ends and no stone

3

unturned, I have been baffled by this story and even faintly disapproving. What right had Jesus to think of himself at a time like this? What right had he to walk away from all those people who *needed* him so much? But walk away he did—not out of indifference or hard-heartedness, but because he needed to renew and redirect himself.

If Jesus can do it, so can we. We're talking about retreat!

To go away by ourselves and rest is not an exercise in self-indulgent escapism, but rather a highly beneficial practice of spiritual self-care. "But I haven't time," we protest. "There's too much to do, too many projects to be completed, too many deadlines to be met. Maybe later, when things are under control...." The good news—or perhaps the bad news—is this: for most of us, things will never be under control. (It is a radical thought— but possibly God doesn't care very much about this particular human obsession.) Moreover, everything will be waiting for us, right where we left it, when we come back. Again taking our example from Jesus, the much-needed retreat is almost always placed squarely in the midst of life's demands, and "real life" is there awaiting our return.

Remember the story of the transfiguration. In many ways this is the ultimate retreat, at least for Peter, James, and John, who have been chosen by Jesus to go apart with him. This is indeed a mountaintop experience! Everything has been changed, and now they see with new eyes. But they return to a scene of swirling activity—pressing crowds, arguing scribes, and a sick boy whom the disciples cannot heal. Here is "real life" with a vengeance. I try to remember this story when I come home from a time apart, physically and spiritually rested and ready to take on the world. In my younger days, this meant reentering the world of children needing attention, a mountain of laundry to be done, and everyone yearning for a mother-cooked meal. (Pizza and hot dogs lose their appeal after a while.) Now it means letters, e-mail, and a pile of pink phone slips demanding response. The descent from the mountaintop is a descent into harsh reality—tedium if not crisis. Our time apart

5

is just that: a limited time of disengagement from the world's concerns to make possible a deeper engagement with God and our own best self.

Typically, a retreat is time away from our workaday surroundings. We might even romanticize the experience a bit and seek out a picturesque monastery or a place of great natural beauty. Most certainly, we are more inclined to prayerful attentiveness in an environment filled with reminders that urge us to prayerfulness. Silence, art, music, ongoing worship by a religious community—these are the "props" of a traditional retreat. I find that I am nourished by being in a worshiping community even if I never go near the chapel! Prayer has soaked into the walls and floats invisibly in the air.

We often retreat to an environment designed to be helpful by its radical simplicity. Most monastic houses offer the simplest accommodations: a crucifix or icon, a bed, a chair, a small desk or table, and a few hooks for clothes. There is nothing to play with! I cannot imagine attempting a retreat in even a modest motel where I would have a television and a phone in the room, for it takes a great deal of strength to keep the world from intruding. Further, most motels (and some conference centers) are simply too comfortable.

Even with spartan accommodations and simple food, a traditional retreat is a luxury. It requires sufficient leisure to get away for a few days. Parish retreats and programs offered by religious houses commonly last from Friday evening through Sunday noon. Two nights away is barely a beginning—I've just begun to quiet down and center myself, and it's time to remake my bed for the next retreatant! Yet even this minimal time apart is more than many of us can manage. Some folks cannot leave their jobs. Those of us with family responsibilities, especially parents of young children and those caring for aged or frail relatives, simply cannot leave their homes. And a traditional retreat also calls for at least modest affluence. There are travel costs, and even the reasonable fees asked by most religious houses can loom large for those with a limited income. Finally, for the homebound—the frail, the ill, and the seriously impaired—travel may be impossible.

For some, the retreat space may bear no special marks of piety. One of my friends shoulders his little tent and supply of food and treks off the beaten path in the Blue Ridge Mountains to find re-creation. Another seeks a special rock on the Maine coast. For me, I know that I have gone apart to a lonely place to rest when I lie on my deck under the Virginia night sky. You don't need icons or crucifixes when you are surrounded by the wonder of creation. But this sort of retreat is also a luxury, calling for the gift of time and access to a gracious space. Even if you wear old clothes and eat your tuna straight from the can, it is not free.

8

Then, too, a conventional retreat can be frightening, or at least provoke anxiety. The seeker— "the retreatant" in classic terminology—may be uneasy about the undertaking. He may regard himself as not holy enough, or feel a little foolish, unsure what to expect. The whole undertaking may seem spiritually pretentious to one who finds nothing extraordinarily holy in her workaday experience, yet feels the unmistakable tug of God. The classic retreat is not everyone's cup of tea.

We need to remember that, after all, the yearning for contemplative time is common, by no means restricted to identified mystics or extreme introverts. Our world is busy, and we are surrounded by *stuff,* much of it good stuff. Like no other people in history, we are bombarded by stimuli. If we were solitary sheepherders or nineteenth-century lighthouse keepers—or, for that matter, tribal people in the Kalahari desert or Inuits eking out an existence near the Arctic Circle—the idea of going apart would seem absurd. We would have no need to seek solitude and clear the clutter from our souls.

I am writing this book for those of you who wish to find the time and space for retreat without ever leaving home. Using the principles of the traditional retreat, we can find ways to build in intervals of reflection and re-creation—not in a concentrated period of forty-eight hours, but spread out over a week or even a month. I hope that much of what I offer will be translatable, and will begin to show you a way to incorporate meditative, re-creative time into an ordinary day. As with any retreat, several things are needful.

First of all, there must be *intention.* Although our intellectual curiosity may be piqued and we may return with an urge to learn more of scripture and our tradition, a retreat is no place for heavy intellectual content. And yet, it is by no means a vacation, or casual, passive time off from work. A retreat is a time to grapple prayerfully with the big questions, to risk the shaking of our assumptions, and to expand our images of God.

Discipline is essential. The retreat has a beginning and an end. As noted, a typical parish retreat or one offered by a religious community lasts from Friday evening through Sunday noon. A do-it-yourself, stay-at-home retreat might better spread out over a longer period—a week, even a month. In that interval, the retreatant sets aside some time each day for quiet, slowing down, solitude, and reflection. This can be as little as fifteen minutes and as much as an hour, but barring an emergency, it needs to be inviolable. It is a good idea to look at your day and notice your most favorable time. You might need to rise fifteen minutes before the family or arrive at your desk before the start of the day's business. Some of us are night people, and our best time is just before sleep. For others, fatigue takes over at night, and it is impossible to concentrate. Look at your patterns and rhythms, and then decide. This is not another tedious chore to be undertaken, but *your* gift to *you*.

You will need a *prayerful place*. We cannot turn our homes into monasteries, and few of us enjoy the luxury of a private chapel or oratory. We can, however, create holy space, albeit on a modest scale. An icon, a crucifix, a candle, a plant on a shelf or table beside our favorite chair can become our retreat house. My own corner has a tape deck (music is for me a powerful aid to prayer), a tiny icon of St. Anne embracing her daughter, and a reproduction of Rublev's icon of the Trinity. Anne has been my comfortable friend for years, and the powerful Russian icon conveys the mystery of the Trinity better than any words. My grandmother's rocker is my *prie-dieu*. (Even as I wrote this, I suspected I might be using this word too loosely and turned to my faithful *Webster's* to look it up. To my astonishment, I found a second meaning: not only is a *prie-dieu* a special kind of kneeling bench, but it can also be "a low armless upholstered chair with a high

11

straight back." That is Grandma's rocker to a T!) Gardeners may have a favorite corner in the garden. Runners can pray as they run.

For a fruitful retreat, you also need a modicum of *privacy.* Securing time alone can be a problem in busy households, especially when not everyone shares the seeker's yearning. Praying is the most intimate of all activities, and the prayer can feel self-conscious, exposed, and uneasy unless some solitude is guaranteed. This might mean getting up earlier or staying up later than the rest of the household. It might mean letting the rest of the family think that you are a little bit crazy. Who knows? Some prayerfulness might rub off.

Finally, a typical retreat provides a *focus,* something to ponder. A good retreat leader does not offer academic instruction, but rather opens doors and raises questions. Scripture commonly provides the needed focus. Almost all aspects of Christ's life—his nativity, his stories of teaching and healing, his passion and resurrection—offer rich material for a quiet time of pondering and prayer. Similarly, a passage from one of Paul's letters or Isaiah's prophecies can draw us deeper into the mystery.

But here I have chosen a psalm. The psalms are, after all, our oldest prayers and songs, a gift from our Jewish brothers and sisters. They lie at the heart of the Benedictine tradition, spiritual forebear of the Anglican tradition. Benedict saw the repeated chanting of the psalms as the work of God: *opus Dei.* His rule prescribes that all 150 psalms be recited each week:

> For those monks show themselves too lazy in the service to which they are vowed, who chant less than the Psalter with the customary canticles in the course of a week, whereas we read that our holy Fathers strenuously fulfilled that task in a single day. May we, lukewarm that we are, perform it at least in a whole week![1]

Contemporary Benedictine worship continues the practice of constant repetition of the psalms, albeit at a more leisurely pace; some communities

13

allow two weeks to complete the cycle, and others a full month.

When we let our imaginations play, this is an attractive picture—cloistered men and women, preferably in picturesque habits, chanting ancient words of the Psalter in Romanesque chapels. In their universality, however, the psalms speak to every one of us. All our human emotions are expressed in them: the noble and the ignoble, the trusting and the doubtful. The psalms are strong stuff, giving a voice to our unacceptable emotions—fear, anger, rage, and the wish for destruction. They are definitely *not* nice. It can come as a surprise to those who know only the gentle and reassuring twenty-third psalm ("The LORD is my shepherd; I shall not be in want") to realize that murderous rage has its place, too. So the persecuted exile, forced to sing the songs of Zion for his oppressor, cries out, "Happy shall he be who takes your little ones, and dashes them against the rock!" (Psalm 137:9). The angry psalms are attractive on the days I want to do everyone in. As one who has spent ample time with the dentist, I can appreciate a curse like "O God, break their teeth in their mouths" (Psalm 58:6). And anyone

who has ever poured kitchen salt on a garden slug
can understand the wish for the enemy to melt
like a snail in the sun. This angry, imprecatory
psalm continues:

> Before they bear fruit, let them be cut
> down like a brier;
>> like thorns and thistles let them be
>> swept away.
> The righteous will be glad when they see
> the vengeance;
>> they will bathe their feet in the blood
>> of the wicked. (Psalm 58:9-10)

15

I'm sure we never learned that one in the Sunday
school of my childhood! We were learning to be
nice.

The psalms speak to us because they are so
human. They begin where we are, in our fallibility
and self-centeredness. They are honest expressions
of need, praise, thanksgiving, fear, and anger. As
Walter Brueggemann states in his highly accessible
Praying the Psalms:

> The Psalms, with a few exceptions, are not
> the voice of God addressing us. They are
> rather the voice of our own common

humanity—gathered over a long period of time, but a voice that continues to have amazing authenticity and contemporaneity. It speaks about life the way it really is, for in those deeply human dimensions the same issues and possibilities persist.[2]

16

The stark immediacy of the psalms calls us into a different place and a different pace. When we let ourselves enter deeply into them, we see ourselves and our world with new eyes. Walter Brueggemann could be addressing us stay-at-home retreatants when he says that entry into the psalms "asks us to depart from the closely managed world of public survival, to move into the open, frightening, healing world of speech with the Holy One."[3]

In this book I invite you to live intentionally and intently for a while with Psalm 62: "For God alone my soul in silence waits." We could dwell just as easily in another. Perhaps a song of lament and abandonment—surely everyone has experienced this anguish, at least now and then: "My God, my God, Why have you forsaken me?" Or a psalm of praise and thanksgiving: "Bless the LORD, O my soul, and all that is within me, bless his holy Name" (103:1). Or a psalm of adoration: "The heavens declare the glory of God, and the firmament shows his handiwork" (19:1). Or one of contrition: "Have mercy on me, O God, according to your loving-kindness; in your great compassion blot out my offenses" (51:1).

17

Yet I am attracted to Psalm 62 as a contemplative psalm. It is a prayer about presence and waiting on God, about living prayerfully and patiently. An everyday kind of psalm, it is not dependent on dramatic circumstances of great joy or triumph or despair. For me, it has been a good companion for the past five years. Like all the psalms, it should lead us—like cows or Benedictine monks—to ruminate. This is a humble and homely activity. As we live with the psalm, we chew on it steadily and find nourishment in repetition. Unlike cows, we may find our rumination to be unsettling. The words that seem so ordinary on first reading may lead us to surprising new places where we encounter God—and ourselves—in new ways.

These eight meditations on Psalm 62 may be read consecutively over the course of a week, or spaced over a month or two. You may wish to experiment with the best approach for your pace and calendar. Although this is not an exercise in scriptural scholarship, reading other translations can sometimes provide new vistas and insights. The quotations in my meditations are from *The Book of Common Prayer,* but translations taken from the *New Revised Standard, New English,* and *New Jerusalem* versions are included at the end of the book. The prayer at the beginning of the first chapter is one I often use, and is offered as another resource during retreat time.

Come away and rest and ruminate! Try to see this psalm with new eyes and hear it with new ears. Play with it, and pray with it. Let it speak to you and live in you.

Gracious God,
mother, father, friend, beloved:

For you alone our souls in silence wait,
for you alone are our place of safety.

You alone are our rock, our shelter and our
refuge, our ever-welcoming home.

In the stronghold of your heart and in the
enfolding embrace of your arms, we are
safe. We cannot be greatly shaken, for you
will not let us fall.

You have spoken and you speak. Open our
ears and hearts and minds to hear you, our
rock of steadfast love.

one

Longing

For God alone...

Freud is reported to have asked, with some exasperation, "What do women want?!" I think the question is more basic and inclusive: what do we, women and men, but first and foremost children of God, want?

It is part of the human condition to want. Babies are born with a reflexive grasp. Adults often find it a winsome trait when a tiny fist closes around an out-held finger. This new little creature likes us, we think, or at least is reacting to us personally. But the action is automatic: the human hand grabs what comes within reach, even before the eyes are clearly focused. As the child develops, the reflex turns into a useful skill. Now the grasping is more purposeful—cookies, Grandpa's spectacles, toys (especially the desirable toys that someone else is playing with). This same grasping infant is uninhibited when vocalizing his needs. When my first child was a newborn, I read a terrifying chapter in Benjamin Spock's *Baby and Child Care* entitled "Unexplained Crying in the First Three Months." Dr. Spock meant to be comforting, but I was dismayed at the prospect of three months—ninety-some days, well over two thousand hours—of trying to figure out what that demanding, loud, but inarticulate person wanted. She clearly wanted *something* and wanted it *now*.

A few years bring focus and relative sophistication to a child. It is a profound spiritual experience to walk through Toys R Us with an uninhibited four-year-old! The prospect of aisles and aisles of brightly colored boxes, promising treasure beyond imagination, is almost too much to bear. There may be a few miniature ascetics among us, but the typical small child wants it all. It doesn't matter what's in the boxes. It doesn't matter that the prize is a tawdry bit of plastic, scarcely more valuable than its attractive packaging.

We become more subtle with age, but the wanting, the need to have something never goes away. My adult equivalent of Toys R Us is the giant bookstore in our shopping center. No matter that I have a stack of unread books at home. No matter that I might even find the books I want at the local public library. The sheer abundance of thousands and thousands of books, acres of them neatly aligned, triggers something in me akin to the reaction of the grabby infant or the greedy four-year-old. I want them all!

Of course, I'm on to myself. I know that I can control myself as I wander through the aisles of Barnes and Noble, that I might succumb and buy a modest paperback at most. I can even congratulate myself that my grasping reflex doesn't extend to mink and diamonds, and that I have never lusted after a Rolls Royce. (There's something meritorious about books, after all. They appeal to *serious* people.) More to the point, I know that at some level this wanting, yearning, needing is a gift from God. It is a gift that can be misused, to be sure, but it is an essential piece of my humanity.

But there is another, seemingly paradoxical side to this: even as we hanker after all sorts of trinkets and treasures, worthy and unworthy, we are acculturated to indirection. Early on, we are taught that it is better not to want, or at least not to want anything too obviously. Women are expected to be self-sacrificing, and men are expected to be self-sufficient, so we lose the spontaneity of the infant and the four-year-old. Our grasping must go underground. Christians especially pick up the idea that niceness is one of the cardinal virtues, and that we must deny or suppress that unscratchable itch to have something. Yet figuratively if not literally, we cannot control the grasping reflex. It must be there for a reason!

To the best of my knowledge, nearly every folklore in the world has some version of the story of the three magic wishes. Without fail the protagonist misuses them and winds up no better and often considerably worse off in the end. Sometimes she speaks heedlessly, squandering a precious wish on a triviality. Sometimes her greed is her undoing: she wants too much and is punished by getting nothing. In all events, the recipient of such divine largesse fails because she simply does not know what she truly wants.

As I was thinking about wanting, I remembered a poetry course that I took in college. Partly, I remember it because I received a B instead of my customary A: it was one of those courses where a photographic memory didn't help. You had to jump in and grapple with the poems, and I hadn't a clue what lay beneath their words. More importantly, though, I remember it because of the professor. She seemed ancient although I realize now that she couldn't have been more than sixty. She looked a little like a benevolent witch or maybe an eccentric fairy godmother. In retrospect, I know that, despite her passion for the Victorian poets, she saw her chief work as keeping her students just a little off balance. One morning she marched into the room and focused her sharp eye on me. "Miss Beltz," she asked, quite out of left field, "are you content?" I was nice in those days, never grabby, and sure that not wanting anything was part of niceness. So I replied, "Yes, I think I am." (It was also part of niceness not to be too forceful.) "Well," responded my teacher, "you might as well be dead." I missed the rest of her lecture because I was pondering my imminent spiritual demise.

My fairy godmother didn't offer me three magic wishes. She just suggested that it was up to me to figure out what I wanted in this life—and to be healthily alarmed if I did not want anything. I couldn't have articulated it at the time, but she was pushing me to look at myself and to figure out what was important to me. What was my passion? And what did I love? What, in other words, did I want?

In our abundant corner of God's world, there is so much to love and so much to be passionate about. In other times and places, when mere survival would be a full-time concern, the lines would be clearly drawn. There would be no impulse to play with the question or to sort out our priorities from the multiplicity of God's gifts to us. But most of us, even when we feel poor, are living in the spiritual equivalent of my giant bookstore. There is much to desire and maybe even more to love.

It can be a rewarding exercise to sit quietly, look deeply into ourselves, and then ask, "What do I truly want?" Initially, we may resemble the four-year-old in the toy store or the squanderer of wishes in the folk tales. I want the biggest piece of cake. I want the window seat on the plane. (Tall folk may passionately want the aisle seat.) I want just a little more money in the bank or more stocks in the portfolio. Our sense that there is never quite enough reminds me of my dachshund of blessed memory, who was sure that she would be happiest walking just six inches beyond the extent of her leash. I want a bigger house. I want to be famous. I want something—I don't know what. I just want. And there is no end of things to want!

So we shift a little and ask, "What do I love?" After all, at a deeper level it is really the same question. I love my family—most of the time. I love my parish church—most of the time. I love my work. I love words and the books that are knit together from words. I love God's creation—cloudscapes unfolding beneath a plane, the brazen little catbirds who beg for raisins at my kitchen window, the wonder of a fresh snowfall. I love a good whodunit and the luxury of a hot shower. I love the amazing newness and perfection of babies. I love the music—Benedictine chant, Argentine tangos, and Schubert *Lieder*— that flows as if by magic from the CD player in my computer. God, there is so much to love in your world!

28

The work of sorting out our desires and our loves is the work of a lifetime. Theoretically, at least, we grow past the comprehensive grabbiness of the four-year-old attracted by bright colors and big boxes. We become discriminating, which means that bit by bit we let go of what does not matter.

For some, this means an ever greater refinement of taste that usually has nothing to do with a yearning for God. Living well—by the world's standards—becomes its own reward. I have friends who are appalled at my willingness to tolerate generic instant coffee. I'm not sure what they would think if they caught me shopping for clothes at Walmart (a turtleneck is a turtleneck, after all). This is not to say that quality does not matter. But relentless pursuit of the exquisite for its own sake can become idolatrous. Or ridiculous.

For us as Christians, however, the object of stripping away the extraneous and defining our priorities is clear. We come to recognize distractions—those actions and ways of being that separate us from God. We come also to recognize our incredible giftedness, the fact that we are surrounded by signs of God's generous presence among us. And we come to realize that God is at the heart of all our yearning, often only after we have determinedly missed the point and sought satisfaction in all the wrong places. Satisfaction sounds like such an ordinary word, but in many ways it says it all: *satis,* enough, and *facere,* to do or make. Ultimately, only God can satisfy. Only God can make enough.

29

The psalmist uses thirst as a powerful metaphor for our yearning, a yearning he identifies clearly as a longing for God:

> As the deer longs for the water-brooks,
>   so longs my soul for you, O God.
> My soul is athirst for God, athirst for the
>   living God;
>   when shall I come to appear before the
>   presence of God? (Psalm 42:1-2)

Jesus, who as a devout Jew knew the psalms, promised the Samaritan woman that he would give her water so that she would never be thirsty again: "The water that I will give will become in [you] a spring of water gushing up to eternal life." She is our sister in her limited, literal understanding: "Sir, give me this water, so that I may never be thirsty or have to keep coming here to draw water" (John 4:14-15).

Like the tired and shopworn Samaritan woman, we are tired of dragging heavy jugs of water in a never-ending cycle of hard work that goes unnoticed and unrewarded. Like the thirsty deer, we are longing for the clear, cool brooks.

We are longing for God, thirsting for God. For God alone.

30

Longing

FOR PRAYER AND PONDERING:

What do I want, truly want?

What desires have I suppressed or denied? Why?

What do I love, truly love? How would I "order" these loves? What is merely liking or attraction?

What can I let go of easily? What should I let go of? What are the loves that define and sustain me?

Augustine prayed, "You have made us for yourself, and our hearts are restless until they find their rest in you." Explore your own restlessness. Maybe you have denied it and need to rediscover it. Maybe it has led you on strange paths—remember, the children of Israel wandered for forty years in the desert before they reached the promised land.

Write, if keeping a journal is one of your paths
to God. Draw. Or take a long, solitary walk,
and talk to yourself—and God.

two

Silence

My soul in silence...

The last time I experienced absolute silence was at the audiologist's. It wasn't painful, but it also wasn't much fun. I sat in a little sound-proof room wearing headphones and straining to hear the first faint sound that was part of my hearing test. Maybe if I hadn't been listening so intently, so uncertain of what the sound would be, and so untrusting of myself that I was afraid that I would cheat just to prove how keen my senses were—maybe if I hadn't been trying so hard, I might have enjoyed the silence. But instead, I experienced it as something negative, something to be broken and filled in as quickly as possible. After all, I wasn't earning any points until I held up my hand, indicating that I had detected a sound. Hardly a spiritual experience, but it made me think about waiting in silence.

34

In *Showings,* the account of her remarkable series of visions, Julian of Norwich talks of putting on God like a garment. It is a homely and appealing picture of comfort and safety. I imagine a favorite roomy sweater, a little baggy in just the right places, or maybe a soft old bathrobe. Who would not want to be wrapped in God, held warmly and securely? Every Fourth of July, when deafening explosions are a sign of celebration and household pets seek shelter under beds and in closets, I remember Julian's image. In our recreational use of noise, we wrap it around us like a blanket. We submerge ourselves in and surround ourselves with sound. We are insulating ourselves—against what?

Sometimes, of course, we are victims. Given my druthers, I would banish "The Little Drummer Boy" from the local supermarket. (He usually turns up around Halloween and disap-

pears abruptly before Epiphany.) Most of the
time, I would rather not be entertained by music
when I am on hold, unless by sheer serendipity
the selection is to my liking. Probably my most
jarring experience as an unwilling recipient of
noise took place at the blood donation center
where I regularly donated platelets. The process,
which takes about two hours, requires that the
donor remain totally immobile. There was something almost sacramental about watching the
plastic bag fill up with life-giving blood compo-
nents. The staff regularly sought to relieve the
tedium by showing movies. Almost without
exception these were loud dramas, filled with car
crashes, assorted explosions, violent chase scenes.
Perhaps I was the only one to sense the irony: if
there absolutely had to be background noise, perhaps Gregorian chant or Beethoven's Ninth
Symphony would have been more suitable.

It is easy to blame society for all the racket,
especially when we live in crowded cities. During
my years in New York, I came to accept noise as
part of the landscape. To be sure, it was often
generated by an assault, a deliberate act of violence. Being awakened by someone strolling

down the street at three o'clock in the morning with a boom box at full volume was annoying, even maddening, but an auditory mugging was preferable to physical violence.

Even when we seek a quiet place, far from city noise, we are surrounded by sounds—planes overhead, cars on the interstate, telephones and beepers. Nature is noisy, too. My neighborhood is patrolled by a flock of criminal-looking, raucous crows. Contemplative silence is out of the question when they choose to perch in the oak tree by the back door.

Yet often we choose noise over silence. Too much quiet makes us uneasy, leaves us feeling open and undefended. I have read that silence falls naturally over a social gathering every seven minutes or so. Every host knows this by experience when the animated dinner party conversation stops abruptly and he or she feels obliged to fill the silence—somehow. Good friends experience this too, but their reaction is markedly different from the nervous response of an anxious host: they are content to sit in the silence and savor it. Perhaps being with God is not so different from being with our best friend. The psalmist urges silence. There is no need for nervous chatter, for this is no ordinary silence.

In the story of Elijah, scripture links silence with going apart to encounter God. The prophet has gone to Mt. Horeb, where "the word of the LORD" comes to him. After Elijah boasts a little of his faithfulness, he is rewarded with the promise that "the LORD is about to pass by." There follows a dramatic display of natural phenomena: first there is a great wind, so strong that it splits mountains and shatters rocks, then an earthquake, and then a fire—"and after the fire a sound of sheer silence" (1 Kings 19:9-12). The voice of God was not in the powerful, potentially devastating phenomena, but in the silence.

I try to imagine the clarity and expansiveness of that silence. Looking within myself, I am baffled and chagrined by my simultaneous yearning and resistance. I am drawn to the intimacy of that prayerful silence, and at the same time I am a genius at avoiding it. The silence of God is not the dead air of the audiologist's little booth: it is living, active, and filled with the Holy Spirit. It is high-voltage. The silence of God demands our surrender. It demands that we shut up and listen, abandoning our defenses and taking off our masks. Elijah, standing outside the cave on Mt. Horeb, must have felt helplessly open, as vulnerable and exposed as a mortal can be. He must have wondered if the wind and the fire would destroy him, if the earthquake would swallow him up.

38

When we let ourselves wait upon God in God's silence, we too become receptive and open. We rid ourselves of nonessentials. Writing of this deep inner silence, Evagrius Ponticus, a monk of the fourth-century Egyptian desert, said that the mind must become naked. I claim no expertise in the fashion world, but I have noted that about every five years the "layered look" is touted as the *dernier cri.* This consists of assorted garments worn one atop the other, with bits peeking out provocatively here and there. The result is a carefully constructed haphazard look. The homeless, who often wear their entire wardrobe at one time, achieve much the same effect.

When we wait for God in silence, we discard the layered look; we strip away the layers one by one. Some are quite elegant, perhaps the spiritual equivalent of a mink coat. Some are beautiful, like a handwoven shawl or an exquisite lace blouse.

Some are warm and serviceable—the tweed jacket that never wears out and seems to improve with age and wearing. Some are purely frivolous—the frilly petticoat just visible beneath the corduroy skirt or the seventy-five-dollar silk necktie. And some garments are tattered and dirty, all too often worn closest to the body. Scarcely visible, they should have been discarded long ago.

Like articles of clothing, our spiritual layers serve to conceal us. We feel safer when our true form is hidden, with curves enhanced or softened, meagerness or obesity disguised. Yet the God upon whom we wait in silence is the God to whom all hearts are open, all desires known, and from whom no secrets are hid. Concealment is not possible. In the words of the old gospel hymn, we come just as we are, without one plea.

To wait for God in silence demands that we pay attention. It demands our awareness of subtlety and smallness. In the silence we become mindful of what might otherwise be dismissed or ignored. We North Americans are a people of superlatives, impressed by the *most,* the *biggest,* the *tallest.* But when we wait on God in silence, we are attuned to the insignificant:

To see a World in a Grain of Sand
And a Heaven in a Wild Flower,
Hold Infinity in the palm of your hand
And Eternity in an hour.[4]

Perhaps most difficult, we must be willing to
get through layers of *seeming* silence to the real
thing. It is relatively easy to stop talking—at least
for a little while—and we can turn off the radio or
the television. Ironically, though, as the actual
sound waves decrease, the inner noise grows in
volume. Sometimes my inner noise reminds me of
the summer cicadas—a rasping drone that
crescendoes, then almost dies away, and finally
comes back louder than ever. This is undifferenti-
ated noise and impossible to ignore, once you
become aware of it. It drowns out every gentler
sound. Sometimes my inner noise twitters softly,
like a flock of small, undistinguished sparrows
settling down for a night's rest in the dense shrub-
bery. The sparrows are more lovable than the
cicadas, pleasant little chirping distractions that
seem harmless enough. Yet they destroy the
silence.

I have become well acquainted with some of
the sparrows who roost permanently in my inner

40

spiritual recesses. They provide the background music of my life, at least until they are drowned out by the rasping cicadas. There is always the noisy distraction of work to be completed and deadlines to be met. (Right now, an almost overdue article—which I should never have taken on—is twittering up a storm.) And there is the nagging chorus of the things that I have left undone and the things that I ought not to have done. I'm not talking about interesting sin, the sort of malfeasance that is the stuff of steamy movies. Rather, I am talking about trivia: all too often, we can let the demands of our daily life become a game of Trivial Pursuit.

Then there are the distractions. These are especially seductive since they can present themselves as constructive. Surely it is selfish to set aside time for silence and solitude when there are so many good works to be done! Surely it is selfish to be preoccupied with my own spiritual well-being when I should be thinking of others. So first I'll deal with this worthy committee or that parish meeting or maybe the collection of food and clothing for the poor—and then I'll settle down for some quiet reflection. It is tempting to say "yes" to everything and everybody and then feel virtuously harassed: there is no time for me because I'm so busy taking care of others. It can't be helped, of course, because God can't manage without me. Even when we are able to let go of our pious and seemingly selfless distractions, the pursuit of silence can be sabotaged by a fleeting reminder to pick up the dry cleaning or make a phone call or take something out of the freezer.

The last harmless-looking but destructive little sparrow is avoidance, what I call "the pencil sharpening syndrome." I know that I am in trouble when I am seized by an urge to dust my study. Even more serious is the compulsion to clean out the messy middle drawer of my desk. The call to silence is strong, but even stronger is my resistance. Like a willful child, I can manage to get *terribly* busy doing all sorts of little tasks that, in the grand scheme of God's economy, do not matter at all.

The prayer of silence is a prayer of listening, waiting, and receptivity. It calls for gentle attentiveness. Those concerned with productivity might see it as the kind of prayer in which "nothing happens," but it is really the prayer of being

Silence

rather than doing in which *everything* happens. For God alone our soul in silence waits.

FOR PRAYER AND PONDERING

When did you last choose silence? How are you drawn to silence? How do you avoid it?

What are your layers to be discarded? What is impeding you and hiding you? What do you need to let go of to experience the freedom to be found in God's love?

How about your sparrows, crows, tree frogs, and cicadas? What are the distracting *inner* noises that fill your spiritual space?

three

Waiting

My soul waits . . .

Our task is very clear: we are to *wait*. To be there. Not to initiate action, but to be on hand. To be ready—for whatever God might choose to do or not do, send to us or withdraw from us. *Semper paratus* could well be the motto, not only of the United States Marines, but of our psalm. Like marines and Boy Scouts, our required stance is one of expectation and receptivity.

When we wait, we live simultaneously in the "not yet" and in the present. There are no short-cuts. Sometimes I think of this psalm when I choose the wrong line at the supermarket: what promised to be a speedy passage turns out to be slow and tedious as the customers ahead of me fumble for the right change and dispute sales items with the checker, who is usually new on the job and struggling with a malfunctioning scanner. My own small plan for my own small life demands rapid and purposeful movement with no wasted time or energy. But here I am, powerless and immobilized, reading the tabloid headlines that Elvis is not really dead or that a farmer in Illinois has grown a two-hundred-pound zucchini. The here-and-now is all there is: an attempt to move to the head of the line or otherwise short-circuit the process would violate an unwritten but powerful code and bring the collective wrath of my neighbors down upon me. Whatever great or trivial things I might wish to achieve in the next few minutes, right now there is nothing to do but to wait.

The psalm, like those frustrating moments in the supermarket line, reminds me of my ultimate powerlessness. Unlike the supermarket—or the airport check-in counter or the freeway toll booth—it also reminds me of the ultimate rightness of that powerlessness. This is not casual, purposeless waiting, but waiting for God. God is in charge. To wait upon God is not a fruitless waste of time or a sign of inefficient, ineffective prayer: it is our God-given work, our assigned task. It is the homework assignment that is never quite completed—at least in this life. It is, of course, ironic but very human to speak of "inefficient" prayer. Most of us want our prayer to accomplish something, to count somehow, or at least to be entered on the credit side of God's ledger. Yet the prayer of waiting is not so much a prayer of accomplishment as one of presence, a prayer of being rather than doing.

This kind of praying requires patience, a vastly underrated quality too often confused with mindless toleration of misery. Yet in scripture, patience is linked with love. As Paul tells us in his first letter to the Corinthians:

> Love is patient; love is kind; love is not envious or boastful or arrogant or rude. It does not insist on its own way; it is not irritable or resentful; it does not rejoice in wrongdoing, but rejoices in the truth. It bears all things, believes all things, hopes

46

all things, endures all things. (1 Corinthians 13:4-7)

Patience is not necessarily an inborn trait. Indeed, the most impatient people I have met are very young infants who haven't a glimmer of what it means to put their wishes or needs on hold for even a short time. I can't remember myself as a screaming, imperious baby, but I know that I learned a lot about patience, not always gracefully or willingly, from my own years of parenting such demanding creatures. Even when the first incredibly arduous months are past, the ongoing primary care of babies and small children is a crash course in letting go of immediate expectations and rearranging priorities.

But for those who have survived or avoided parenthood, life continues to offer myriad opportunities for learning. In other words, life continues to challenge us by forced confrontation with our own limitations. I do very well when I can choose my own "opportunities for spiritual growth," but confess to considerable anxiety as to how I will cope when—not if—my patience is tested by the growing helplessness of old age. I suspect that there is some point at which the tests of true patience become very real. Physical frailty and forced immobility may well make continued virtuous faking impossible.

Even though patience is rarely noticed and even more rarely rewarded, at least in worldly terms, it can be heroic. There is nothing short-term about it, and the end is not always, indeed rarely, apparent. While there is always a purpose in our exercise of patience, the fruits can be elusive. Whether we are waiting for the tomatoes to ripen, our child to reach maturity, a new language to become fluent—or whether we are waiting for God, our patience is grounded in hope.

Waiting without hope is empty and futile. Only the assurance, however faint and wavering, that our patience will be somehow rewarded sustains us. We wait willingly and patiently on God because we are promised that it will be worthwhile; we are assured that we will be comforted. This promise echoes through the psalms:

O tarry and await the LORD's pleasure;
be strong, and he shall comfort your heart;
wait patiently for the LORD.

(Psalm 27:18)

Further, we will profit if we wait patiently: we will possess the land while "evildoers" will be cut off (Psalm 37:10, 36). This assurance appeals to my primitive sense of justice: not only will I get my share, but the bad guys will be deprived! So we wait patiently upon the LORD, confident that he[5] will stoop to us and hear our cry (Psalm 40:1). Moreover, we wait eagerly, with our attention sharply focused:

> I wait for the LORD; my soul waits
>   for him;
>   in his word is my hope.
> My soul waits for the LORD,
> more than watchmen for the morning,
>   more than watchmen for the morning.
> O Israel, wait for the LORD,
>   for with the LORD there is mercy.
>   (Psalm 130:4-6)

In other words, our waiting will not go unnoticed by God. Even when God feels distant and we feel lonely or even abandoned, we are waiting in the context of his enduring love. The image of the night watchman is powerful for all who have ever sat bleakly through the darkness of a long night. We know that morning will come—at least we are pretty sure, since dawn has always come before. Yet this night feels unusually long, and maybe it is like no other night. We wait patiently and in hope, but we can't be quite sure until we see the first steak of light. So we fix our eyes on the horizon and strain forward to catch the tiniest glimmer.

50

The watchman's stance is one of constant, unrelenting attentiveness. Whether he expects the dawn to bring good news or disaster, his work is to watch. I would be tempted to add some undemanding chore to his watch: at the very least, he could polish boots or shell peas while keeping his eyes fixed on the distance. Surely he could be expected to do more than merely stand there; surely this seemingly empty time could be filled more profitably. But such attentive and attuned watchfulness is not an emptiness, even though it might feel like one. Rather, there is a powerful concentration of energy when we wait in awareness of the promise.

The picture of the watchman waiting for the morning is deceptively simple. True, only the most inept would look resolutely to the west for the rising sun. Yet when we wait upon God we can find ourselves confused or distracted, looking in the wrong direction. Or we might grow tired or bored, and then be tempted to suspend our watching—just for a little while. Death has been the traditional penalty for falling asleep on sentry duty. Most of us will never find ourselves in such drastic circumstances, but we have all experienced the chagrin of wandering attention or looking in the wrong direction. I rejoice that ours is a God of Second Chances!

One of my icons for the kind of attentiveness demanded by God is the experience of watching for the teller's light to come on when I wait in line at the bank. Besides my own desire to get it right, I feel pressure from the people behind me: they are all in a hurry and will have no patience with a bumbler who doesn't move at once in the right direction when the light flashes. So I watch, ready to jump at the right moment.

Ordinary watching and waiting can be tiring and discouraging. Even as we wait upon God, we can lose sight of the promise of hope. Hope, Emily Dickinson's "thing with feathers," can, after all, be elusive. When we feel that our faithfulness is unrewarded, we may well cry out with the psalmist:

> I have grown weary with my crying;
> my throat is inflamed;
> > my eyes have failed from looking for
> > > my God.   (Psalm 69:4)

52

Not only do I grow weary, I have a gift for missing the point. With the psalmist I can maintain steadfastly that I am waiting for God, which sounds quite grand, but I can easily lose sight of what I am about. What does it mean, anyhow, to say that this is the work of my soul, overshadowing everything else in my life? What does it mean to dedicate myself to waiting and watching?

There are powerful clues in the gospels. When Jesus commissioned his disciples, he instructed them, "As you go, proclaim the good news, 'The kingdom of heaven has come near'" (Matthew 10:7; see also Luke 10:9). To the questioning scribe he said, "You are not far from the kingdom of God" (Mark 12:34). And when the Pharisees asked him when the kingdom of God was coming, he answered:

> The kingdom of God is not coming with things that can be observed; nor will they say, "Look, here it is!" or "There it is!" For, in fact, the kingdom of God is among you.[6] (Luke 17:20-21)

So we watch and wait for something—someone—that is already present. We live in the present and the future, and the tension between them can exhilarate or confuse us in turns. Sometimes we are so intent on peering into the far distance that we fail to scan the near foreground. Sometimes we miss the tiny, humble signs of God's presence because we are expecting the spectacular.

And sometimes we savor our waiting. After all, many of the best times of life are times of waiting. Small children grasp this when they first understand the joy of opening the little windows on the Advent calendar not all at once, but day by day as they count down to the Feast of the Incarnation. Women know it as they await the birth of a wanted child. Somewhere I still have the desk calendar I kept as I waited for the birth of my daughter. Carefully, I crossed off each day— not because I was in a hurry or because I saw the pregnancy as an unproductive prelude to the "real thing." Instead, each of those 280 days of waiting was remarkable, to be experienced fully. I was living on a threshold, a physical and spiritual space that simultaneously reassured me and filled me with awe. I was living both in the present and in the future.

In the fourteenth century Meister Eckhart, who I am sure knew nothing about real, flesh and blood babies, preached three compelling sermons about the birth of God in our soul. He understood about patient and hopeful waiting, just as he grasped the analogy to human birth. The change at first is imperceptible. No one notices. Even the mother is not sure: Is it true, or do I imagine it? But the growth of new life is inexorable and not always smooth. There are spiritual parallels to the unpleasantness of morning sickness. The wait can even seem like movement in the wrong direction, away from life. One of the early signs of pregnancy, after all, is excessive sleepiness: new life is springing from apparent dormancy.

Mary knew about this joyous and perplexing waiting for new life. I imagine that she savored it: the surprise of the first barely perceived flutter of movement must have been no different for a young mother in first-century Palestine. I imagine that she wearied of it, too, as her body grew heavy and clumsy. Yet even without the angel's announcement, she would have known the holiness of her waiting.

Mary's life reminds us of the symmetry of waiting: she also knew about waiting at the other threshold. She knew about the time that is simply to be endured, the passivity that calls for the heroism of resignation. Her hours of watching at the foot of the cross were a terrible waiting, the antithesis of the months of secret joy of carrying her child within her. When I feel very brave, I try to put myself in her place, at least in my imagination. Was she tempted to curse God? Did she want time to speed up or slow down? Did she remember the angel, the shepherds, and the magi? What was it like to wait for God with the incarnate God dying before your eyes?

Maybe she remembered the psalm. Maybe she found inner silence in the midst of turmoil and knew that her soul waited for God alone.

For Prayer and Pondering

Think about your times of watching and waiting, those times in your life when the night was dark and God seemed distant.

Think about those times when your watching has been rewarded.

Have you ever spent a long time looking in the wrong direction? What reoriented you?

Have you ever watched at the foot of the cross?

four

Imagining

God alone is my rock . . .

When I was a child, I pitied grownups. For a lot of reasons. They spent too much of their time sitting around and talking. They never ran, and they hardly ever sat on the floor and played. They had no toys, at least nothing that I would identify as a toy. (Now I know better!) But they were most to be pitied for the dreary books they read. Big books with *no* pictures! How, I wondered, could they possibly find any joy in black and white pages with no pictures?

I still like picture books, but now I know that books, good ones anyway, and especially the Good Book, are filled with pictures. When the psalmist says that God is his rock and his stronghold, he is not saying that God is a geological formation or a fortified building. Rather, he is offering us a picture, *one* picture of the essentially unknowable God. Like the familiar anthropomorphic personifications—king, shepherd, judge—it is a true picture, albeit a partial one. It can bring us a little closer. It can help shape our prayer. It can fire our imaginations.

I know that I was drawn to this particular psalm because I love rocks. I love to look at them and hold them, running my hand over their smoothness and their sharp edges. I love the coolness that comes from deep within them, even on the hottest days. I love their mystery, how they carry the story of ancient plants and animals in their fossils and the story of earth's shifting and settling in their layers. My friends know all this, so they bring me rocks as presents. One carried a sizeable black rock home to me from Wales, a mark of real devotion if her suitcase was packed as tightly as mine usually is. Another recently brought me a shell filled with tiny rocks from the Maine coast, no two alike. Yet another delighted me with a Petoskey stone, smooth and gray, marked with an intricate pattern of ancient fossils. These stones are found only in upper Lake Michigan, remnants of a coral that lived 350 million years ago when the area was a tropical sea. When I hold the Petoskey stone in my hand, it feels as if I am holding a little piece of the first morning of creation.

"God is my rock," says the psalmist, inviting me to loose my imagination and look around my study at my treasures. A Petoskey stone or a tiny bit of mica from the rugged Maine coast? Or maybe a geode, split open to reveal sparkling crystals? Maybe a rock too big to be contained, even in this spacious room.

The landscape that I know most intimately and love most deeply is a few acres of the Virginia Blue Ridge in Rappahannock County, where the soil has worn thin so that there are great rock faces and outcroppings. Farmers of earlier times must have found it a harsh and grudging land as they almost literally scratched out a living. Now the chief crops are apples and cattle, and the craggy hillsides have returned to woodland. Jenkins Hollow, however poor it might have been for raising corn, is rich for God-imagery. Rocks are everywhere! A rocky ridge rises behind the old house, and the fast little mountain stream in the front yard is filled with rocks, too. The huge boulders seem immovable, yet I have heard them rumble down the stream in flood time and waked to find the river rearranged during the night. The force of the water has polished the smaller rocks that line the streambed. In the water, they are brown and white, reddish and slate blue. The colors change and fade when the rocks are dry. Surely there's a message here: mutability and immutability are all mixed up, and things are not what they seem.

Whenever I read this psalm, I can picture my favorite rock outcropping on the hill behind the house. It is immense, simultaneously simple and complex, seemingly changeless yet always in the process of subtle change. It is smooth, gray-black. A few seedlings have taken root in the crevices where leaves and pine needles have softened its hardness. My rock retains coolness in summer and soaks up the sun's warmth in winter. In the spring thaw, water oozes mysteriously from its unbroken surface. Is this what it was like when Moses struck water from the rock? Maybe it did not gush; maybe it just trickled out slowly and gently.

When I perch on the mossy ledge at its base and lean against the rock, it feels solid, immovable, seemingly eternal. I feel safely hidden, although if anyone bothered to look up from the hollow they could probably see me. I look across the hollow and the line of trees to Sam's Ridge. The sky up here is huge, much bigger than in the hollow. I watch the turkey buzzards as they swoop and glide in search of carrion. They are amazingly graceful birds in flight; met face to face as they devour rotting flesh, they are menacing and ugly. There's a message here, too: I am alone, but not really alone, in the presence of beauty, power, and a touch of terror. And possibly I need to revise my idea of what is ugly in God's creation.

"Set me upon the rock that is higher than I," prays the psalmist (Psalm 61:2). Take me to that safe place that is like no other. Show me your picture.

I know that God is infinite, eternal, and unchanging—and my rock is not. But that rock is a picture, an image, a metaphor that expresses my yearning for safety and a sense of God's presence. That rock tells and shows me something about God that even the most eloquent words and compelling logic fail to do.

Within our corporate worship, God-imagery is well-defined, if not consciously prescribed, in the language of the prayer book and hymnal. The most common metaphors are God as shepherd, Jesus as the good shepherd, and the creator God as king and judge. Statues and windows in our worship spaces also present comfortable and familiar visual images—again we see the shepherd and the king. We see God incarnate as a lovely human infant and God incarnate as a broken man on a cross. We see God as Christ in majesty, God as the risen Christ. For over a decade my seat in the seminary chapel faced a stained glass window of the resurrected Jesus. I could never look at it without smiling. Perhaps unintentionally, the Victorian Gothic artist had depicted a risen Lord who looked for all the world as if he were disco-dancing! It was an especially welcome sight on spring mornings after the solemnity of Holy Week. Who wouldn't dance after being liberated from the cold darkness of the tomb?

I suspect that, for many of us, Michelangelo created the definitive picture when he painted the ceiling of the Sistine Chapel: God as Father-Creator—majestic, powerful, male, and definitely not to be trifled with.

In our solitary, meditative prayer, other images may arise. These are inner pictures of a piece of God, fragmentary but truly our own. We may ignore them or fail to recognize them. Especially in dreams, they come unbidden. Sadly, we may try to censor the imagery that wells up within us, repressing everything that doesn't seem "appropriate" for prayer or doesn't fit our idea of God as received from *The Book of Common Prayer* or, more likely, the Sunday school of our childhood. We miss so much when we try to curb our imagination! It is just possible that God is trying to tell us something.

I never met Margaret Wise Brown, the author of several gentle, deceptively simple books for children, but I suspect that she tapped into rich inner resources of God-imagery. My particular

favorite is *The Runaway Bunny,*[7] which occupies
a place of honor in my modest theological library.
For those who do not know the book, it is the
story of an adventurous little rabbit and his mother. Whenever he announces that he will run away,
his unflappable, all-loving mother replies that she
will follow him. If he becomes a fish, she will
become a fisherman. If he becomes a rock, she
will be a mountain climber and climb to where he
is. If he becomes a crocus, she will be a gardener
and find him. That indefatigable mother bunny—
God?— has an answer for everything. Finally, the
runaway capitulates and announces, "Shucks, I
might as well stay where I am." "Have a carrot,"
says his mother. I had read that story myriad
times with my children and my grandchildren
before one day it dawned on me: this is Psalm
139!

> Where can I go then from your Spirit?
>   where can I flee from your presence?
> If I climb up to heaven, you are there;
>   if I make the grave my bed, you are
>   there also.
> If I take the wings of the morning
>   and dwell in the uttermost parts

> of the sea,
> Even there your hand will lead me
> and your right hand hold me fast.
>> (Psalm 139:6-9)

Further, we can so easily overlook the wealth of imagery in the Bible, especially in the psalms, and in the tradition of the church. We get locked into an idea of what is "proper" or "correct," seeing God's very gifts of imagery and imagination as dangerous distractions. Even in scripture, when yet another picture of the unknowable God painted from a new angle with fresh colors turns up, we avert our eyes and slip past quickly instead of lingering to savor. So Isaiah offers us the compelling picture of God as a nursing mother, a delightful and surprising contrast to Michelangelo's fierce patriarch:

> Can a woman forget her nursing child,
>> or show no compassion for the child of
>> her womb?
> Even these may forget, yet I will not
>> forget you.   (Isaiah 49:15)

The psalmist suggests a maternal God who invites us to climb into her capacious, welcoming lap:

> But I still my soul and make it quiet,
> like a child upon its mother's breast;
>> my soul is quieted within me.
>> (Psalm 131:3)

I find this psalm especially comforting on the days when I am out of sorts, overworked and under-appreciated—in short, mad at everybody. God is allowing me, a shopworn septuagenarian, to be an obnoxious toddler. God is saying, "Go ahead and have your snit. I'll just hold you for a little while until you feel better, and then you can climb down and play nicely."

As an observant Jew, Jesus knew the psalms and their imagery; he must have remembered the prayer "Hide me under the shadow of your wings" (Psalm 17:8) when he lamented over the city of Jerusalem:

> Jerusalem, Jerusalem, the city that kills the prophets and stones those who are sent to it! How often have I desired to gather your children together as a hen gathers her

brood under her wings, and you were not willing! (Matthew 23:37)

A few years ago this image was incorporated into one of the trial eucharistic prayers authorized for use by the Standing Liturgical Commission. There were amusing ripples of outrage from folk who did not know its scriptural roots. What irreverence, they protested, to talk about poultry at the Holy Table!

One of the most appealing images for me is not scriptural, but part of the piety of the Middle Ages: Christ as pelican. According to the legend, the father bird revives his dead young by piercing his own breast and letting his blood flow over them. It is a wonderfully mixed-up picture: we are nourished by the blood of Christ as a child is nourished by his mother's milk. We are restored to life by his self-sacrifice, just as we are brought to new life in the waters of baptism. The pelican is simultaneously mother and father, life-giver and restorer. In the same chapel that has the disco-dancing risen Christ, there is a worn mosaic in the floor right behind the altar: a eucharistic pelican piercing three holes in her breast, her blood dropping into the mouths of three very alive young birds. I always felt grounded when I stood within the circle of that mosaic.

In Luke's gospel, Jesus gives us another picture that shows us something new about God. Tucked between the familiar parables of the lost sheep and the prodigal son is the story of the anxious housewife (Luke 15:8-10). When she discovers that one of her ten precious coins is missing, she tears the house apart until she finds it. I have seen numerous windows and pictures of Jesus tenderly carrying the lost lamb on his shoulder and of the prodigal being welcomed joyfully by his father, but I have yet to encounter any picture that shows God as an anxious housewife. Yet this surprising bit of imagery greatly expands our vision as it gives us a new and homely glimpse of God's unrelenting care.

We tend to be protective of our God imagery, confusing image with essence. Then too, any departure from the familiar is unsettling, and we are reluctant to push out the limits and expand our vision, especially where personal or community piety might be challenged to stretch a bit. Yet I am convinced that we are invited to play, pray, dream, and meditate about our inner pictures and names for God. We might at first be reluctant for fear that God will somehow zap us if we let our words and minds stray from traditional images drawn from the prayer book and our childhood prayers. If we are mindful of the wealth of imagery in scripture, however, we know that there is treasure waiting to be discovered; there are new landscapes asking to be explored.

For Prayer and Pondering

As we enter another time of quiet and reflection, I invite you to be attentive to your images of God. What do you call God? How do you image God?

For that matter, what does God call you? Does God have a pet name for you? Or a rather stern appellation that makes you sit up straight in apprehension?

How does God image you? What does God see when God looks at you?

five

Enemies

They seek only to bring me down...

In other words, just because you're paranoid, so the cliche goes, doesn't mean they aren't out to get you. God may well be the rock-like source of salvation, but almost all of us, at one time or another, have been convinced that the bad guys are out there plotting to do us in, in great ways and in small. Never mind that there is no rational basis for our fears, never mind that we are not so powerless and abandoned as we picture ourselves, never mind that our active and creative imaginations have been working overtime. Never mind, for that matter, that our fears might be well-founded.

> How long will you assail me to crush me,
> all of you together,
>> as if you were a leaning fence,
>>> a toppling wall?
> They seek only to bring me down from
> my place of honor;
>> lies are their chief delight.
> They bless with their lips,
>> but in their hearts they curse.
>>>> (Psalm 62:3-5)

These verses leave me feeling lonely and frightened, as if I had heard the cry of one small and friendless person facing overwhelming odds. *Everyone* is out to get him, eager to topple and crush him. They remind me of one of the singsong chants of my childhood passed on by oral tradition that was strangely comforting on those days when I felt left out and despised by all:

> Nobody loves me,
> Everybody hates me,
> [I'm] going out in the garden and eat
> worms.

I have no idea why it felt so good to feel so bad, why there was such consolation in seeing everyone else on the playground as the enemy. Maybe when we yield to pervasive paranoia, at least the lines are clear: it is a matter of *them* and *us,* with no confusing gray areas.

The psalmist presents us with the quintessential enemy, one who wants to crush and discredit us, one who seeks our bodily and spiritual destruction. This is a devious enemy, delighting in lies and deception. And, of course, the big question is this: Who is the enemy? Maybe the psalmist is mistaken, overanxious, and fussy— there is no enemy beyond his own fears. Like a frightened child at bedtime, he has seen monsters in the shadows and is sure that God-knows-what is lurking under the bed. Or maybe the enemy is real, and he is in mortal danger, physically and emotionally.

Sometimes the enemy is not a person at all, but merely the convergence of harsh circumstances. It is an old truism that trouble comes in threes. Certainly, anyone who has been diagnosed with a major illness, lost a job, and been abandoned by a loved one—all in the space of a few weeks or even months—can't help but feel targeted by some malevolent force. On a smaller scale, there are those days when we oversleep, get stuck in traffic, and discover that we are wearing mismatched shoes.

It is harder to identify and confront the enemy who is faceless and impersonal, an oppressive system that grinds us down and threatens to quench the God-spark within us. Poverty can crush us. Debt can crush us. An endless cycle of repetitive, meaningless work can crush us. It is no accident that inmates of Nazi concentration camps were kept busy moving piles of rocks across a field and then moving them back again, compelled to work at an unrelenting pace. The meaninglessness of the exercise only added to its cruelty.

After all, to repeat the cliche: Just because you're paranoid doesn't mean that somebody isn't out to get you. We might add: Just because you wait faithfully on God doesn't mean that you won't encounter danger. Nor are you guaranteed freedom from enemies.

Some of us find it nearly impossible to accept the fact that not everyone wishes us well. My three-year-old grandson John Ross let out a yell of shocked disbelief when a wasp had the temerity to sting him. His sense of betrayal was almost more painful than the sting itself. "Why," he asked through his tears, "did it want to *hurt* me?" He had wished no harm to the wasp, indeed had scarcely been aware of its presence. With indiscriminate malice, at least from his viewpoint, it had left him with an angry, throbbing welt. Since then he has been mildly paranoid about hovering winged creatures who seem especially attracted to him, but otherwise, he has retained his trust in the essential goodwill of others.

Maybe the enemies are like John Ross's wasp, coming out of nowhere with no visible provocation. Sometimes we are simply in the wrong place at the wrong time when a wrath-filled person with the need to crush *someone* comes along. As "road rage" enters our vocabulary, drivers are learning to be careful not to antagonize their fellows. Who knows where a casual gesture of annoyance or impatience might lead?

But perhaps there has been provocation on our part, and we have been too inattentive to notice. I experienced this not long ago at the post office when I bypassed a fellow customer and beat him to the window. I hadn't even realized that he was in line. He was convinced that I had taken something from him, if only a minute or two of his time, and that I had done so intentionally. It was a trivial incident: no blows were exchanged, and even our conversation was relatively civil. It reminded me, however, of my skewed perceptions. I am highly conscious when I am being *done unto*. But absorbed in myself and convinced of my customary benevolence, I can be utterly unconscious of the impact of my actions (or inactions) on others. Those of us who are basically trusting and well-intentioned know the feeling of shocked betrayal when we then experience unexpected hostility. "What did I do?" we ask. "What have I ever done to him?" We can persuade ourselves that our injured innocence is justified, but it usually contains at least a few drops of egotism.

It is scarcely realistic to assume that everybody loves us, especially if we are honest enough to admit that *we* do not love everybody willy-nilly. It is certainly not realistic to assume that we have never hurt or irritated anyone, even inadvertently, especially if we remind ourselves of the times when we have "nobly" overlooked slights and petty hurts, proud of ourselves that the perpetrator never suspected how he had offended—or that he was more or less forgiven. Nevertheless, I am always surprised when I encounter envy and ill will. "Why do they want to hurt me?" I ask like the psalmist. "What have I ever done to them?"

At the other end of the spectrum from the trusting optimists are those who live with a sense of pervasive, chronic mistrust. They assume that the enemy is everywhere and that life is a battlefield, if not a never-ending guerrilla war. They are not surprised that "they"—whoever "they" are—seek to crush them and bring them down. Devastating as it is to be surprised by betrayal and hostility, I prefer to live expecting only good, but I number among my friends and colleagues good folk who live in constant awareness of the enemy's malevolence. These are frightened and joyless people whose lives become a self-fulfilling prophecy as their fear communicates itself to all who encounter them.

Tiger, the German shepherd who belonged to my neighbor in Jenkins Hollow, was sure that the world was out to get him. Since I prided myself on my St. Francis-like ability to win the trust of animals, even the least likeable, I was sure that all he needed was a little love: a few pats, an assurance that he was really a splendid animal, and maybe a handful of dog biscuits. So I set out to win Tiger. He would accept the food warily and sometimes even let me scratch that delicious place behind his ears. "Great," I would think, "we're making progress. He just needed a little reassurance, but now he knows that at least I am his friend." But the very next day, Tiger would look at me as if he had never seen me before and growl with raised hackles and menacing stance. As I negotiated a dignified retreat, I wondered if St. Francis could have done better.

Tiger was a dog, and not a very admirable dog at that. I do not know what experiences in his puppyhood made him so sure that the world was populated with people who wished him harm. At worst, he was a nuisance, adding a disagreeable note to otherwise pleasant walks. But his human counterparts are tragic.

Most of us are born expecting good things from those around us. To be sure, there are inborn differences of temperament. Some babies are all smiles, reaching out to friend and stranger alike, while others are naturally more cautious. But for most of us, at least in this ofttimes abundant and gracious corner of God's earth, the world is a friendly place. Yet sooner or later, we all encounter someone who assails us to crush us. Like my innocent grandson, we encounter the human equivalent of the aggressive wasp. In the right circumstances, any of us might cry out, "How long will you assail me to crush me, all of you together?" Although the psalmist does not supply the background or develop the story, his main point is clear: God's steadfastness and reliability are his stronghold when faced with the hostility and deception that surround him.

The message here is that, despite exemplary faithfulness and unswerving trust in God, life is not smooth. We encounter anger, treachery, and hypocrisy on a small, personal scale in our own lives but also nationally and globally. I recall my mother, who had lived a sheltered life with no sense of enmity beyond a neighborly sparring with the woman next door with whom she was in polite competition about husbands' income and children's achievements. As quite an old woman, she happened to be visiting me during the Cuban missile crisis in 1962. It is difficult for younger generations to imagine the fear that enveloped and threatened to paralyze us in those difficult days and weeks. (This was during the period when folk were building bomb shelters in their backyards.) "But Baby," my mother would say, calling me by my hated family name, "surely no one would want to harm the United States!" The idea of such impersonal and devastating enmity was incomprehensible to her.

It is easy now, as it was then, to yield to pessimism, to feel surrounded by "yous" and "theys" bent on our destruction. Mutual mistrust mocks our national pieties: we pride ourselves on openness, generosity, and good will—and yet we live in a state of anxious disquiet. Are we ready for whatever might come? Can we really trust the Russians or the Chinese? Or for that matter, can we trust each other—Republican or Democrat, black or white, male or female? When I sit with my coffee at the kitchen counter and read the morning newspaper, it is easy to feel besieged and even easier to relinquish trust in a society that excels in half-truths and verbal manipulation. "Lies are their chief delight"—all kinds of lies, ranging from blatant falsehoods by political leaders to the blandishments of the advertising industry.

It is easy to feel helpless and hopeless until we recall that these dark verses are not the entire psalm, but rather are a somber note in a song of trust and hope. Despite the imagery of crushing and toppling, we are not helpless. Our first task is to identify the enemy. It helps to know what we are up against. Otherwise we contribute to the destructiveness by irresponsibly casting blame in all directions. After all, it can't be our fault if "they" are out to get us. Sorting things out makes self-pity and excuses more difficult. So we need to clarify and define. Otherwise the enemy takes on the creepy omnipresence of menace in a B-grade movie, where a slimy, malevolent something oozes under the door and simply takes over.

So who *are* they? Who are those who assail us to crush us, who seek to bring us down? They are those who envy us; those who want what we have or, failing that, for us to have it no longer. Those whom we have hurt, intentionally or inadvertently. Those who fear us. Those who feel only contempt toward us. Those who are inexplicably filled with hatred: maybe we have the wrong skin color, the wrong gender, or the wrong sexual orientation. Maybe we happened to be in the wrong place at the wrong time.

This is hard news. The world has not changed a great deal since the psalmist paused in his song of trust to complain of those who threaten him. Much of the time, however, in this largely affluent and privileged corner of God's world, we live out our lives in relative security. The assaults on us are not fatal: vicissitudes rather than tragedies, bumps rather than killing blows.

It may come as a surprise to realize that there is an enemy closer to home than the violent random killer, the scheming con artist, or even the thoroughly unpleasant person at the next desk. The twittering sparrows and rasping cicadas of distraction are not the only inhabitants of our inner space. A coterie of destructive little adversaries dwells within us, assailing us to crush us and seeking to bring us down. These enemies are harder to identify than the foes that appear on the six o'clock news. Maybe the ubiquitous "they" have made a comfortable home within us, blocking our growth and keeping us from getting what

we truly want. We can blame our cozy inner
enemy for our discontent. Nothing then is our
fault: the system, the government, the neighbors,
the multinational corporations, the health care
industry are out to get us.

Even more insidious are the mocking little
voices deep within us. Among them are self-doubt
and its close cousin, self-contempt. What mas-
querades as humble self-effacement is often a
denial of our God-given gifts. Garrison Keillor
tells the delightful story of his aunt, an expert
baker who talked the judges out of awarding her
first prize for a superlative cake at the county fair.
"It's not so good as the one I baked last week ... it's
too moist ... it didn't rise high enough ... I don't
know, it just didn't turn out right." By the time
she had finished with this rambling critique of her
masterpiece, the judges were convinced that it
wasn't such a great cake after all, and his aunt
was spared the challenge of celebrity. So we tell
ourselves, "I can't. It won't work. I'm not smart
enough. I'm too old. I'm too young. It will cost
too much. It's never worked before. There's no
use trying. I'm just a housewife." In so doing, we
kill vision and creativity; we smother a tiny spark

of divinity before it can begin to glow. We let ourselves be crushed. We collude in our spiritual deadness:

> For my enemy has sought my life;
> he has crushed me to the ground;
>> he has made me live in dark places like
>>> those who are long dead.
>>>> (Psalm 143:3)

83

In the realm of enemy voices, fearfulness is a close relative of self-doubt and self-contempt. We persuade ourselves that it is better to stick with the tried and true. As the old Scottish saying puts it, "Better the devil you know than the devil you don't." Change for the sake of change and risk for the sake of risk can be foolish and imprudent. But unwillingness to stretch and risk and grow is also a kind of death wish.

When as a child I first heard the story of the ten talents, I identified with the deficient servant who had missed the point completely (Matthew 25:14-30; see also Luke 19:12-27). I was sure that the only reasonable and responsible course was to hold on tight to what I had been given and hide it in a safe place until I was called to account. I remember my astonishment and discomfort at the idea that the money was to be used to make more money and that the resources were expected to increase. What if the bold servant who invested his five talents had made a bad choice and lost them all? What on earth could he say to the boss at the day of accounting? And was it worth bothering with only two talents? There's not much margin for error there. Better to play it safe! I was confusing risk with recklessness. Timidity stunts us spiritually and makes us meager in every way. Our attempts at generosity are not generous, but rigid and perfunctory. Joy is beyond us, and celebration an alien concept. True compassion is too costly. Saddest of all, our image of God is small and circumscribed by our fearfulness. Fearfulness is another killer!

Coldness of heart is another enemy that can hide in our inner recesses. While the zeal with which assorted saints are reported to have kissed the sores of lepers seems excessive, no one could accuse them of closing their eyes and their hearts to the suffering of others. I, on the other hand, can fool myself by calling my coldness "impartiality" or "objectivity," thereby creating a comfortable buffer zone between myself and the suffering manifest around me. I can steel myself not to notice, and I can smother any little stirrings of imagination that threaten to disturb my complacency. Coldness of heart, like fearfulness, can protect me from the costly work of compassion.

Then there is hypocrisy. The psalmist says of his enemies, "They bless with their lips, but in their hearts they curse" (Psalm 62:5). These are not the merciful little social lies that spare pain and keep things running smoothly—"No, I'm happy to sit in the middle of the back seat; these compacts aren't really crowded at all" or "That haircut is really just fine—and of course it will grow out before you know it!" Rather, the psalmist describes deep deception: the smiling face and uttered blessing conceal a murderous heart. Even when we are not literally capable of murder, we can bless with our lips and curse within our hearts in small and hurtful ways.

Finally, there is falsehood: "Lies are their chief delight." We are not born with a love of truth. Small children lie because they cannot tell the difference between truth and falsehood. Before we are very old, though, we lie because we don't want to get caught. We lie because we want to look good—shame can be a powerful force pushing us away from truth. Any of us who has shaved away ten or fifteen pounds when reporting our weight knows about this kind of falsehood. We lie for gain. Even upright citizens walk a narrow and slippery path, especially around the day income taxes are due to be paid. We lie because we fear we won't be liked or respected if we are known without embellishment. I now find it an interesting bit of family history that Great-Uncle Will did time for stealing a horse. He was a clumsy criminal—it was his brother-in-law's horse, and he didn't get far with it. There was a time, however, when I expunged him from the family tree: surely I merited a more elegant bloodline! Those of us who are *technically* impeccable truth-tellers manage to lie skillfully by omission. We are truly in danger when we come to believe our own lies.

This is grim news! Indeed, these troubled and troubling verses stand in sharp contrast to the confidence that pervades the psalm. It is as if our limited, human voice interrupts: "Wait a minute! What about all that's wrong in the world, the enemies without and the enemies within?" It is a voice that must be heard, if we are to be honest.

FOR PRAYER AND PONDERING

Take some time to identify some of your inner enemy voices. How do they divert you from exercising your gifts? How might you diminish their persuasive power?

Jesus said from the cross, "Forgive them, for they know not what they do." What does forgiveness mean? How do you forgive those who have hurt you?

How do you forgive yourself for hurts you have brought upon others?

six

Refuge

*[God is] my stronghold, so that I shall not
be greatly shaken.
Put your trust in him always, O people,
pour out your hearts before him, for
God is our refuge.*

By the time I was ten, I was a fluent, greedy reader. I had my own little stack of children's books that I read over and over. By the standards of our modest neighborhood, this was a treasure trove, but it was not nearly enough to satisfy my appetite. So along with the *King James* Bible, I satisfied my hunger for the printed word with *The*

Kansas City Star. With World War II on the horizon, the front page was filled with maps and charts detailing the relative strength of armies—the number of tanks and horses, men and planes. Even when the numbers were discouraging, I was reassured by glowing accounts of the Maginot Line, a massive system of fortifications that was to keep the Nazi forces from overrunning France. Surely all would be well. For all of Hitler's posturing, his menacing armies would be contained. Evil could and would not triumph, even temporarily.

Sheltered as I was, thousands of miles and an ocean away from the threat of war, I wanted everyone to be safe. Altruistically, I wanted people in the path of the tanks and guns to be spared violence and destruction. Although I could not articulate it, more selfishly I knew that their supposedly impregnable defenses would fail to save them, and that no one was really safe—if not from jack-booted invaders, then from unknown, unseen forces. I was surprised and disappointed when the Maginot Line turned out to be a bad joke. The invading armies simply went around it! This was an important spiritual learning, although

I didn't label it as such when I was ten years old. Maybe the world wasn't so safe after all.

It is part of the human condition not to feel very safe. But ideally, at one time, we all felt secure. I have no clear recollection, but I am inclined to believe the psychoanalysts who tell us that we all carry pre-birth memories of life in the womb as a place of ultimate safety. The fetus is cushioned, gently carried, and protected from shock. In conditions of hardship, it continues to be nourished even as the mother's body is depleted and starved. How like the work of a maternal God to design a fetal life of protection and plenty with extra privileges for the tender new being!

It is essential, too, for infants and small children to continue to feel secure, safe in the care of people who love them. Neglectful deprivation is less dramatic and brutal than intentional abuse, but nearly as harmful—and potentially fatal. Babies who are not held, cuddled, and talked to are sad babies. They fail to thrive, and can suffer irreversible damage or even die. Whether they are born into mansions or hovels, whatever the externals, their world is not safe.

I am reminded of a story, quite possibly apocryphal, that illustrates our human vulnerability and the necessity of loving nurture, not because it is "nice" to feel secure, but because a minimal sense of safety is essential for life. It is the story of an experiment ordered by an absolute ruler with an inquiring mind: in one version, the ruler is the medieval emperor Friedrich of the Holy Roman Empire, in another it is James I, and in yet another it is a legendary, nonhistorical king. Whoever he might have been and whenever he might have lived, this powerful ruler had pondered what the language of the angels might be and decided to address the question scientifically. He procured some newborns—almost everything is possible for an absolute regent of whatever century—and ordered that they be brought up in a laboratory-like nursery. They were to be fed adequately and to be kept warm and clean. Their caregivers, however, were enjoined to avoid all speech, indeed all unnecessary physical and emotional contact. Uncorrupted and unconfused by human discourse, the babies were expected to begin to speak spontaneously in the angelic language. Instead, they died, unloved in a world that was not at all safe. Their carefully designed nursery was neither stronghold nor refuge.

In our superior knowledge, we can smile at such naivete about how God's great gift of language is imparted while we rue the sacrifice of babies, even apocryphal ones. But the story is a powerful reminder that we cannot grow and thrive, physically and spiritually, unless we feel safe. Not perfectly, not totally, perhaps unsettled at times—but essentially safe. I am sure that this is why newborns are so daunting, why our hearts *should* drop to our stomachs when that tiny bundle is put in our arms at the hospital door and we are sent on our way with a godlike responsibility. It is clear now that babies are not born with a latent angelic language somewhere in their nervous systems, nor are they born with a theological system just waiting to be developed. They learn about being human and they learn about God from the hands that touch them and the voices they hear.

For those blessed with a gentler and warmer beginning than our babies in the story, the idea of an all-loving, all-caring God is not incomprehensible. Even imperfect parents—and all are imperfect— provide a glimpse of God's perfect love. For those of us not so blessed, we can at least *imagine*—wistfully? angrily? yearningly?—what it might be like to be held safely and tenderly. We all yearn for that first, safe home where we were carried gently and shielded from hurtful jolts. We all want to go home. We all want to be safe.

Before we are very old, we no longer feel very safe. Yet the yearning for safety always is there, so we build ourselves bunkers—literal and figurative. And they are illusory, like the impregnability of the Maginot Line.

We are very good at creating comforting illusions of safety. In New York, my kitchen windows had massive bars, put there to protect me from the burglars and assorted felons who, I was sure, were lurking just outside. They probably kept the bad guys out of the kitchen, but they did nothing to tame the demon of insecurity that threatens all of us. Now I live in a gentler place, a neighborhood where the bars have been replaced by official-looking signs in front of each house: "Protected by BES."[8] I'm sure that BES is an efficient company, but I am less sure that I can rely on the security it promises. The system challenges my technical skills as I program it for my absence, just as it challenges my physical agility as I dash through the door to disarm it in the nick of time when I return home. Occasionally, it has whimsical moments when out of nowhere it whoops, "Intruder! Intruder!" More to the point, I am not really sure what it would or could do should a real, live bad guy turn up in my kitchen or bedroom. So I have turned off the system and left the signs. They make me and my neighbors feel that we are holding all manner of destructive forces at bay.

We work at building our Maginot Lines: prudent foresight can even become an obsession. Surely, we think, nothing bad can happen to us if we have adequate life insurance and have found the right medical plan. Surely we will lack for nothing if we invest wisely in real estate and engage in sound financial planning. Surely no bodily harm will come to us if we have state-of-the-art bars on our windows or a few of those protective signs planted strategically on our lawns. Some of us seek safety in our work, our professional identities, or our carefully structured plans for achievement. I hold mortality at bay by seeing my dentist twice a year and working out on my Nordic Trac. Surely I will never die if my teeth are well cared for and my blood pressure low! I look with a touch of envy at my monastic brothers and sisters, convinced that they find safety in the rule, the common times of prayer and silence, and the haven of the convent or monastery. No doubt Gothic architecture and the lingering scent of incense can be counted on to hold all harm at bay. Maybe that's why I always sleep so well on a retreat! But of course, I'm just a guest so I am permitted the luxury of illusion. In my heart I know that, spiritually, real life in a monastery is no safer than real life anywhere else.

It is a hard learning to accept the fact that all our efforts at creating security for ourselves, however prudent they might be in worldly terms, are at base illusory. We need only to look at history or the daily news to know that the fabric of our everyday lives is *very* thin. On a global scale or on the smallest, most intimate scale, it can be ripped apart—torn open in a moment. At a routine physical, I blithely give access to assorted cells and bodily detritus. Examination of those few cells can bring reassurance or devastating, life-changing news. As I settle back with a glass of wine and wait for an indifferent meal to be served "when we reach cruising altitude," I try not to remember that an inexplicable mechanical failure can send a giant airliner plummeting into the Atlantic a few miles from the airport and a few minutes after takeoff. Corporate restructuring can render productive workers "redundant," a bland word that masks spiritual violence. That the decision is made impersonally does not lessen the pain. Storms, floods, and earthquakes show us how frail our human structures are and how undiscriminating the destructive forces of nature can be.

Long after the bombing of the World Trade Center and reports of the plot to blow up the Lincoln Tunnel under the Hudson, I find that I try to blot those memories from my mind when I must be in similar places that are ideal targets for impersonal rage. "It's just better not to think of our vulnerability in tunnels or planes or tall, crowded buildings," I tell myself when the sub-way train stalls between stations or a shifty-look-ing character boards the plane. Then I work hard at the impossible task of *not* thinking about the possibility of destruction, however far-fetched it may be. Yet the daily news reminds us that no place is exempt from the threat of impersonal rage: schools and offices no longer feel like safe places, and the perpetrators of random violence look remarkably like our friends and neighbors. Farther from home, the safety of daily life is crumbling for people in former Yugoslavia, which not so long ago was being promoted as the ideal spot for carefree tourism. Indeed, no corner of the earth can promise tranquility if we let ourselves look beyond our own small circle and at least try to absorb the stories of devastation that flood the media.

The psalmist tells us that *God* is our stronghold, our fortified place, and surely more reliable than iron bars on the windows or a stockpile of weapons. God is our stronghold, so that we shall not be *greatly* shaken. Adverbs are usually dispensable, but this is an important little word. We are not promised that everything will automatically be just fine, painless, or easy. No, we are promised that, with God as our stronghold, we shall not be *greatly* shaken. But we *will* be shaken—this is part of the human condition. Lady Julian knew this six hundred years ago. She could have been paraphrasing this verse when she wrote the familiar words: "He did not say you will not be troubled, you will not be belaboured, you will not be disquieted; but he said: You will not be overcome." That's the important part: we may be shaken, but we will not be greatly shaken. Our safety may seem threatened, but we will *not* be overcome.

We are promised safety with God, for God is our refuge. We are safe because the relationship is loving and intimate. The psalmist says, "Pour out your hearts before him" (Psalm 62:9), an invitation to childlike openness. Most of us have been socialized to pour out our hearts before no one. Despite the availability of psychotherapists and spiritual directors, we are—perhaps correctly—unwilling to let ourselves be totally open, totally vulnerable, and totally known. Even the people who love us and who live in close proximity with us have been given an edited version and only know us imperfectly and partially. But with the God who gives us safety it is possible to be entirely open. It is impossible to be otherwise! Remember the collect for purity, our prayer of preparation before the eucharist, when we address the God to whom "all hearts are open, all

desires known," and from whom "no secrets are
hid" (BCP 355). Not all our desires and secrets
are laudable, or even presentable. Yet we can
pour out our hearts because—in all our imperfec-
tion and wrongheadedness—we are nevertheless
known, loved, and accepted as God's beloved
children.

99

It is not easy to trust. As children many of us
begin to learn not to trust, and those early lessons
are amply reinforced. Our national credo might
well be: Don't expect much, and you won't be disappointed. All too often, we carry this attitude
into our prayer, whether from a mistaken belief in
"niceness"—God will figure it out, but it is more
polite for us to be indirect—or possibly because
we do not take prayer very seriously. But there is
the example before us of Jesus' encounter with the
blind beggar Bartimaeus. Remember it? He is sitting by the road as Jesus and his friends pass by
on their way out of Jericho. He calls out, "Jesus,
Son of David, have mercy on me!" The people
around him try to hold him back, to keep him
from making a nuisance of himself. After all, he is
a throwaway person. But Jesus stops and says,
"Call him here." Then the mood of the crowd

changes, and they say, "Take heart, get up, he is calling you" (Mark 10:46-52).

It should be obvious what Bartimaeus needs— maybe some new clothes, maybe a decent job, maybe healing from his infirmity. Almost any small gift of kindness would be welcome. But Jesus asks him, "What do you want me to do for you?" He almost forces Bartimaeus to ask for what he needs, to acknowledge that he *wants* something, indeed to pour out his heart. When I picture the scene, I can imagine Jesus being willing to stand there for as long as it takes, maybe all day, until he gets a straight answer to his question, "What do you want me to do for you?" He doesn't want to hear, "Whatever you think," or "Anything that isn't too much trouble," or "Nothing really, I know you're busy, and I have no business taking up your time."

Some of the things we pour out might be shocking, surprising, or distressing. We tend to be ashamed or frightened of our own rage. And the very idea of being angry with God—or at least dropping our guard so that God might notice our anger—is shocking! Prayer is supposed to be dignified, restrained, *polite*. But "pour" is not a subtle word; it is prodigal and generous. There is nothing half-hearted about pouring. Think of rainstorms: when it pours, we are drenched. The psalmist tells us that we open our hearts, not drop by drop and bit by bit, but completely. We hold nothing back; we let our fear, hope, sadness, anger, uncertainty, and joy all pour out, secure in the knowledge that we are held safely and securely.

This verse reminds me of another psalm about trust, one especially dear to me and already cited. We can easily overlook it because it is so short, but in a quiet way, the psalm is about pouring out our hearts to God:

> But I still my soul and make it quiet,
> like a child upon its mother's breast
>   my soul is quieted within me.
>   (Psalm 131:3)

Scholars tell us the "I" who speaks here is not an infant, but a little child. Think about toddlers—wiggly, headstrong little people, incapable of dissembling. When they have temper tantrums, their rage and grief are so total that they seem unreachable. When they feel safe, they nestle like soft little animals. Maybe this is how God sees us, at least some of the time. Very small children are wonderfully adept at pouring out their hearts when they feel safe. And they feel safe in their mother's arms and on her lap.

The God who is our stronghold is the God who holds us like a good mother and invites us to whisper our secrets in the safety of that holding. The God who tells us we will not be greatly shaken, that it will be *all right*.

FOR PRAYER AND PONDERING

Try to remember yourself as a small child. If you can't remember, use your imagination! Then recall the invitation to nestle close in God's capacious lap and to pour out your heart. What do you want to say? What have you been afraid to say?

What do you yearn to let go of? What secret joy do you want to share? Remember: in your prayer this is a safe place. Become a heedless toddler, at least for a little while.

seven

Weighing In

Those of high degree are but
a fleeting breath,
even those of low estate cannot
be trusted.
On the scales they are lighter than
a breath,
all of them together.

When I lived in Buenos Aires thirty-some years ago, I bought my fruits and vegetables from Sam the *frutero*. Around eleven o'clock every morning he would move slowly down our street in his old green pickup truck, the back end

piled high with oranges and tiny, bright red straw-
berries, slightly tired-looking apples, and all manner of greenery. I would come out with my basket
and select the day's supplies. Paper or plastic bags
were an unnecessary frill so the *habichuelas* jos-
tled happily together with the *cebollas* and the
cerezas in the basket. Sam supplied language
instruction along with the vegetables, responding
patiently to my *Como se llama?* with the name of
the item in question. He even gave cooking tips
for anything completely unknown to me. He
weighed the produce in a simple, hand-held scale,
adding to the empty pan from his collection of
weights until both sides were perfectly balanced.
Laboriously, after each balance was achieved, he
wrote a number on a scrap of brown paper and
presented me with the total at the end of our
transaction.

I haven't seen a scale like Sam's for decades.
But the psalmist is talking about just such a deli-
cate system of balances when he warns of mis-
placed trust and false values. The attractive
distractions of the worthless and the ephemeral
are "lighter than a breath." Heaped on the scales,

their weight does not even register, and the pans remain strikingly lopsided.

These are the uneasy, uncomfortable verses. When I am meditating on this psalm, wrestling with it and chewing on it, I am tempted to skip over them. I have been feeling so good: God offers me rock-like safety and immutability. God invites my unquestioning trust. God promises that I will not be greatly shaken. And now, abruptly, I am pulled back to the uncertainty and discomfort of so-called real life.

The tone is cynical: "Those of high degree," we are told, "are but a fleeting breath." Surely there was no cult of celebrity when the psalms were composed, but the words are prescient. Now we are surrounded by the images and utterances of those of high degree of one sort or another—political and military leaders, entertainers and athletes, the stupefyingly wealthy, all the rich and famous whose only claim to fame is their celebrity. We scarcely need the warning of the psalmist as we assiduously mythologize and then demythologize, canonize and then topple our secular saints. The cycle is old, yet the game is ever new: we keep creating new little false gods only to destroy them. I have given up trying to keep abreast of the current media idols. It is either a sign of advancing age or gradually developing wisdom, but they all have begun to look pretty much alike. They are indeed disposable, a fleeting breath.

Sometimes I think about Sam's scales as I wait in line at the grocery store, especially when the tabloids lined up by the cash register catch my eye. How much would Yassir Arafat weigh on the scales? How many weights would be needed to balance the British royal family? Or Elvis, recently sighted yet again? Or all the New York Yankees and the Dallas Cowboys, scrunched together on one side of the scale? What about Martha Stewart and Donald Trump? If we are to believe the psalmist, their collective power, wealth, celebrity, and athletic skill count for very little in the great scheme of things.

At the same time, the psalmist also allows for no romanticizing or idealizing of those "of low estate." They too cannot be trusted. Those of us of tender conscience can become sentimental—and patronizing—toward those whom we perceive to be our inferiors. But whether we are as generous as Mother Teresa or as grudging as the unreformed Scrooge, we all have our categories by which we define ourselves and others. "Everyone diminishes someone," in the trenchant words of Iris Murdoch.

Who are my people of low estate? The homeless woman who sits on a bench every day by my bus stop, unwashed and mammoth in her obesity, surrounded by bags of old newspapers, seemingly unreachable. The young mother and her "boyfriend" whose pictures look back at me from the morning *Post*, stolidly confessing the abuse and murder of a child. All the violent, angry men who fill our prisons. The hundreds, the thousands who have the misfortune to be in the path of an earthquake or flood, whom I dismiss because their sheer numbers defy my mind's grasp. All those whom I judge as useless or dangerous or merely faceless—I use them to assure myself that *I* matter, that on God's scales I weigh more than they do. Despite our wish to see victims as somehow ennobled by their victimhood and malefactors as larger than life in their wickedness, the psalmist reminds us that they too are merely human—and not to be trusted. No one is exempt.

On the scales, we all weigh very little. Indeed, practically nothing.

At best, we are all flawed and limited. And we are all mortal. This message is powerfully apparent in a popular genre of late medieval art, "The Dance of Death." The stylized paintings of this era are a grim reminder of our human limitation: Death is depicted as a grisly, grinning skeleton, holding hands with a cross section of society. Bishops and kings join hands with housewives and farmers as Death leads them in the dance.

Nowadays the line would have movie stars and TV anchormen, home run hitters and high-fashion models, politicians and televangelists mingling with the ordinary folk. I can't imagine a contemporary Dance of Death in my dining room, nor would I want to look at it every Sunday in the church down the street. But the message is clear, even if we avoid disturbing visual aids: no matter what the bathroom scales may say, none of us weighs very much. Our souls may be immortal, but our bodies—along with our accomplishments and acquisitions—are impermanent and quite expendable.

Weighing In

I would rather not know this. At least I would like to think myself exempt from the inexorable message of God's scales. While I occasionally wondered whether Sam's weights were to be trusted, I have no doubt at all about the accuracy of God's scales. It is absurd to think that I can pad the numbers a little, the reverse of what I did years ago on a helicopter flight. To balance the load on the aircraft, each passenger was required to announce his or her weight, which was then repeated loudly for everyone in the line to hear. I suspect that I was not the only person to shave off ten or so pounds—and to mumble at that. Yet life is no helicopter trip, and ours is the no-nonsense God for whom alone my soul in silence waits. This God, who knows my weight already, would not be impressed by my optimistically adjusted number. God is God, and I am not God. Everything that I want to hold on to is lighter than a feather in the wind. I, self-absorbed and self-important, weigh nothing. I, seeking God and—as my mother would say—meaning well, am lighter than a breath.

I thought I knew this, but it came to me as fresh news a few years ago when I last met with the teacher who had been my mentor since I was seventeen. Although we saw each other rarely, we had stayed in touch over the years. He occupied a special place of respect and affection in my heart, where he never aged or faltered. When my travels took me to the university town where he had lived for nearly fifty years, I found him in a nursing home, sitting in a wheelchair at the edge of the group, watching vacantly while a bright young woman led the residents in songs. Then for a few wonderful minutes he knew me. He held my hand and said, "My dear little girl" over and over again. I was sixty-something and he was nearly ninety. He had never shown such feeling when I was his student; indeed, he had been demanding and sometimes unreasonable in his expectations. I had been no one's dear little girl for a long time, and I knew that no one would ever call me that again. He soon lapsed into confusion and introduced me to a passing aide as his mother-in-law. My challenging teacher, larger than life and never at a loss for exactly the right word, was revealed as *very* mortal.

Back at the hotel, I shed tears because he was dying, but my greater sadness was for myself.

They were good tears. In a thirty-minute visit in a
rather elegant and relentlessly cheerful nursing
home, I had glimpsed mortality: my teacher's and
my own. More to the point, I was overwhelmed
with an awareness of the transience of all things.
Toni's life—after decades I was finally able to use
his given name—had been rich and full. He had
inspired, indeed ignited, a love of learning in
countless students. In its own way, my life was
equally rich and full. I was blessed with work that
I loved and a warm circle of friends and family.
Yet I knew, as I held his hand in the dayroom, that
we were lighter than a breath, both of us together. Made in God's image and precious in God's
sight, we were nevertheless sojourners. Our com-
bined 150 years of living and achieving barely
tipped the scale.

Astronauts train arduously to prepare themselves to experience weightlessness. Traveling in
space, they demand that their bodies act and react
in unnatural ways. Mentally and physically they
must accept that "up" is not necessarily up and
that "down" is not necessarily down. They let go
of the comfort of firm ground beneath their feet.
When I look at the grainy pictures of bizarrely

suited figures floating near the ceiling of the spacecraft, I wonder: Do they feel light and free? Or do they feel adrift and disoriented? Is it fun, or does it make them nauseous? Do they feel powerful, or do they feel helpless?

Despite John Glenn's geriatric foray into space, I doubt that I shall ever experience the physical phenomena of weightlessness. I suspect, however, that there is great freedom in accepting my spiritual weightlessness, my nothingness on God's scales, once I loosen my grasp and let my feet leave the ground. Letting go of all that seems valuable, putting those of high degree and those of low estate in their proper perspective, calls for a mighty leap, a seemingly reckless abandon.

I remember myself, decades ago, as a novice skier. I wasn't very good; in fact, I was terrible. But I stayed upright most of the time and distinguished myself by plodding sturdily back up the slope after an unsteady descent. (This was the cheapest hotel to be found in the Tyrol, so there was no lift; students in the early fifties expected no such amenities.) Then one night the instructor waxed my skis and didn't bother to tell me. I can still feel the terrifying, exhilarating *Whoosh!* as I took off down the slope. There was nothing to hold on to. I had been forced to let go. I was not in charge, and it seemed not to matter. It was *all right.*

There is a final tough message in this portion of our psalm, one that sums up the cautions and prohibitions of the preceding verses: "Though wealth increase, set not your heart upon it" (62:12). This is hardly an argument against prudent foresight. It is reasonable to plan for the future: resources for education, health care, retirement cannot be taken for granted. But here, as always, it is a matter of perspective and proportion. There is great comfort and healthy pleasure in sufficiency. After all, we pray regularly that God will give us our daily bread, whatever we need to sustain us. The Jesus who comes to us through the gospels is a provider and feeder. He provided abundant food for multitudes, he ate with his friends, and he accepted the hospitality of all sorts of people, from despised tax collectors to community leaders. Those who disapproved of him called him a glutton and a drunkard. He was certainly no advocate of harsh deprivation. Our peril comes when we do not know when we have enough, when we forget that all is gift.

In the *Jerusalem Bible*'s translation of this verse we are counseled: "Keep your heart detached." Easier said than done! True detachment is something much deeper and more difficult than simply not caring. Jesus suggests this when he urges his friends to live in such a way that the right hand does not know what the left hand is doing:

> But when you give alms, do not let your left hand know what your right hand is doing, so that your alms may be done in secret; and your Father who sees in secret will reward you. (Matthew 6:3-4)

In other words, we are to be profoundly aware of our actions and at the same time unaware, unselfconscious. T. S. Eliot says much the same thing in his poem-prayer "Ash Wednesday": "Teach us to care and not to care." We care deeply, but at the same time we are able to separate ourselves—detach our hearts—from all that is less than God.

114

Weighing In

How might you practice experiencing spiritual weightlessness?

Packing for a trip—even a short one—is a powerful spiritual experience. Most of us want to take along too much, just "in case" we might need it. How would you pack your *spiritual* suitcase, light enough for you to carry easily and small enough to fit into the overhead compartment? What do you truly *need* to sustain you? What do you leave behind? In other words, what truly nourishes you and what weighs you down?

What are the ten most important things—people, possessions, intangibles—in your life? Make a list, rank them, and then prayerfully imagine letting go of each in order of its importance.

eight

Listening

God has spoken once,
  twice have I heard it,
    that power belongs to God.
Steadfast love is yours, O Lord,
  for you repay everyone according
    to his deeds.

Even in my heydey, I was never an inspired pianist. My playing was conscientious and workmanlike, and most of the time I could hit the right keys. But while my piano-playing bore a marked resemblance to my accurate typing, my inner experience of creating music was something else. I particularly loved the challenge of Bach fugues and could practice them tirelessly, weaving my way through the tangled lines of melody, never quite sure that I would emerge triumphant from the maze. It was always an adventure. Even if I had more or less mastered a piece, after the first few notes I felt as if I were jumping off into the unknown, rich with promise and fraught with confusion. Then at the end of the piece, the strands would come together, and the work would close with a great satisfying chord. This resolution of all the voices always took me by surprise, and I would feel a tiny surge of triumph. Chaos and discord had not prevailed after all!

Like a Bach fugue, the lines of melody in our psalm have come together in a harmonious chord. There are no new pictures, no more seeming digressions, and no further shifts of mood or viewpoint. The God for whom we wait in silence is addressed directly for the first time. And that God is not impossibly remote, but on speaking terms with us. Still.

This is not always comfortable, for ours is a high-voltage God. As the writer of the letter to the Hebrews tells us:

> Indeed, the word of God is living and active, sharper than any two-edged sword, piercing until it divides soul from spirit, joints from marrow; it is able to judge the thoughts and intentions of the heart. And before him no creature is hidden, but all are naked and laid bare to the eyes of the one to whom we must render an account. (Hebrews 4:12-13)

Ouch! Whenever I read these words, an image rises unbidden in my mind, a homely image from the kitchen. I think of boning a chicken—how the very sharp, slim knife slides through the flesh, dividing joints from marrow cleanly and decisively. It is a radical, indeed a surgical process. Of course, the image can't be pushed too far: the quite dead chicken is being prepared for the oven and has no future. We, on the other hand, fully alive and challenged to grow and change, are being reminded of the intimacy and intensity of our relationship with God. We are able to withstand the scrutiny of the God who knows us so thoroughly because we are assured of his love.

The God who calls us into such close and loving relationship has truly spoken to us in scripture and *continues* to speak—in the liturgy and in our prayers. Our waiting on God, then, requires ongoing attentiveness if it is to be more than an empty exercise in passivity. When we pay attention, our awareness is sharpened. Then we hear God speak, predictably in sacred settings, but also in wildly unlikely places and circumstances: the subway, the shower, and the messy garage. After all, the Holy Spirit is blowing over us all the time, sometimes as gentle as a baby's breath and sometimes roaring like a Kansas tornado.

God speaks to us in the seemingly chance words of friend or stranger. God's voice can be heard too in the words that appear to leap from the pages of a book, often words that we have read many times and think we have exhausted. We hear God's voice in our dreams, if we let ourselves be open to them. We hear it in "what we always knew," when the ordinary gains the sudden clarity of insight. God's voice is powerful in the arts and pervasive in the book of nature. As St. Ephrem wrote in fourth-century Syria, "Everything in creation points to the creator." It is all a matter of paying attention.

We need, of course, to be careful. The annals of crime and psychology are filled with stories of the misguided and demented who have claimed a special channel of privilege. But when we listen for God while we are at the same time held securely in the container of the Christian community, we are protected from arrogance and delusion by scripture, the sacraments, and the candor of our friends who love us well enough to speak truth to us.

"God has spoken once," says the psalmist, "twice have I heard it." This is a jarring note: God speaks *once,* and we hear *twice!* The reverse is true in our ordinary family conversation. Just think of all the feeble jokes about husbands murmuring, "Yes, dear," to anything their wives might say, all the way from "How about pasta for supper?" to "I'm thinking of joining the Foreign Legion." In our human discourse, we expect many false starts and much wasted effort. There's no need to struggle to get it right the first time—you'll have ample opportunity to hear it again. The ultimate experience of hearing many utterances for one message is, for me, the telephone answering machine. When the caller is a fast-speaking mumbler, I may be forced to play the tape two or three times to catch a number or a name. The unseen voice speaks thrice. Once—if I am lucky—have I heard it.

God's discourse is different. One succinct utterance bears two distinct messages that seem at first glance incompatible: power and steadfast love belong to God. Am I really hearing two things, or do they belong together? Yet if the wolf and the lamb can lie down together, maybe power—especially the power of the God who knows our innermost being—and love are joined in harmony.

I confess that I am uneasy with power. Somehow power isn't nice. Well-brought-up women and other polite Christians supposedly resist it—or at least act as if they do. I'm happy to accept the mysterious, obedient power of the combustion engine that moves me swiftly down the highway or through the air. And I am delighted with the equally mysterious power of electricity that lights my house, enlivens my computer, and washes my clothes and dishes. I know too that, untamed and unharnessed, this power could

121

kill me: hence, the wisdom of approaching downed power lines with the utmost caution.

The power manifest in nature is impersonal and awesome, and even more mysterious than anything devised by human hands and minds. As I write, my part of this country is gripped by the most devastating drought of the century. Fields and lawns are brown. Trees shed their leaves in midsummer. Little streams have simply disappeared, and the Hazel River has become an insignificant creek. This is less dramatic than the raw force of a hurricane or earthquake, but nevertheless awe-inspiring. It is humbling because it reminds us of our insignificance in the great scheme of things: we can create and achieve and accumulate on a grand scale, but we cannot make it rain. The promising clouds that appear from time to time are taunting reminders of our human powerlessness. They seem to say, "We'll release the moisture when we're good and ready, but you may have to wait for a while."

All power ultimately belongs to God, the psalmist says, but God clearly doesn't keep it all to himself. It is here, in our world, accessible to us. Yet even as we are attracted to power—personal, political, or emotional—we resist it, for possession brings with it responsibility for its use and lays bare our capacity for evil. So long as I have no power, I am not accountable. Then I can lament corruption and violence. I can be frightened and outraged at the destructive forces loose in our society. I can place everything negative and hurtful *out there* somewhere. I can even blame God for being an inefficient hypocrite: if God *really* has all that power, why doesn't he do something?

It takes resolution and courage to embrace those bits of power that God sends our way even though we might prefer to be passed over. There is scriptural precedence for such diffidence. Jeremiah demurred, "Ah, Lord GOD! Truly I do not know how to speak, for I am only a boy" (Jeremiah 1:6). Yahweh's rejoinder was terse: *Don't give me any excuses. You'll go where I send you and say what I tell you to say.* Similarly, Moses offered abundant excuses for refusing God's call: *No one will listen to me, no one will believe me, and besides, I'm not a good speaker.* Again, the LORD is tough: *Just do as I say! I demand your cooperation, which means your working with me and sharing my power. Don't worry: you'll manage just fine* (Exodus 3-4).

124

As awesome as hurricanes and nuclear fission may be, as heady as our own little forays into taking charge may be, ultimately all power belongs to God. Such pure power is beyond imagination: I no more aspire to encounter God's undiluted power than I wish to loiter at ground zero of a nuclear explosion. Yet the psalmist inextricably links this terrible power with steadfast love, a high-voltage love as overwhelming and inexplicable as God's power. It bears no resemblance to infatuation, fondness, or the saccharine affection celebrated by the greeting card industry. Rather, it is the enduring and unshakable love of a covenanted relationship, simultaneously demanding yet tolerant, for God continues to put up with us regardless of our shortcomings and our straying from the path. God's love is unwavering and unchanging.

Jesus talks with his friends about God's overwhelming love and reminds them that they have experienced it directly: "As the Father has loved me, so I have loved you; abide in my love" (John 15:9). It seems too simple: if we are able to love, we *know* God. Moreover, if we obey Jesus' commandment to love one another, God *abides* in us and we *abide* in God. That's an old-fashioned sounding word, one we don't use often, certainly not outside the church. But think about it: if we love, God lives in us, God abides in us, God moves in permanently. There is nothing skittish or haphazard about "abiding." God is there to stay, the God who *is* love.

And there is another important point about love, something we have heard often, maybe even know in our heads, but forget so easily once we close the Bible. God's love is so powerful and expansive that it leaves no place for its hurtful, destroying opposite: fear. Fear is unholy; fear keeps us from God; fear itself can become a false and devouring god.

I wonder how many of our sinful ways of being and doing can be traced back to our fear: our fear of failure, our fear of change, our fear of growth, our fear of all that is *other*. The fruits of our fear are bitter: violence, spiritual deadness, and contempt toward all whom we would push to the margins. I suspect that most of our sinful *isms*—racism, sexism, ageism—are the fruits of fear.

God's love for us is without "because." It is an *event,* a fact made manifest in the awesome fact of the incarnation. And for us in our human limitation, there is only one "because" when we speak of God and love together: we love because he first loved us. We love because of God's love, revealed to us in his Son. Anything else is flawed, contaminated and hampered by conditions and stipulations. False and harmful sometimes, bland and possibly pleasant other times—but not really love.

God is love. I know that is so because it was written up on the wall of my third-grade Sunday school room. I've been hearing it all my life, and I believe it (although sometimes I may act as if I have forgotten it). God loves me. God loves you. God loves us. I know that is so, even though I work hard at forgetting it all too often. "Whoever does not love does not know God, for God is love" (1 John 4:8). If we are to be God's children and Christ's friends, we *have* to be lovers—not selective and picky lovers, but wildly expansive, letting our love reflect the prodigality of God's love.

126

Can we do it? Maybe. Especially if we remember that God's love fills the space between us, so that we are not separated but bound together in Christ. And that God's love abides in us, simultaneously constraining us and setting us free.

Steadfast love and power—yes, they *do* belong together, complementing and completing one another. Love unsupported by power is weak and ephemeral, and power without love is terrifying in its potential for harm. Yet linked, they give us a glimpse of God. For a moment, I think that I hear the majestic, satisfying chord that binds everything in our psalm together in harmony. But then, in the last verse, there is a disturbing ambiguity. Finally, the psalmist—with all of us—speaks directly to God: You, the all-powerful and all-loving, will repay us all according to our deeds. Is this a threat or a promise, or perhaps a little of both? Has the loving relationship been reduced to a business arrangement of credit and debit, or a demeaning system of reward and punishment? Maybe that final harmonic chord isn't so conclusive after all. At the very least, it feels as if a dissonant note has been introduced, leaving us off-balance and uneasy.

Here biblical scholarship can be helpful, especially to us amateurs. It tells us that the Hebrew word translated in *The Book of Common Prayer* as "repay" has its root in the rich, promising Hebrew word *shalom:* God's peace. Here is a third note to make our satisfying, triumphant chord rich and complete: we are not merely compensated for our efforts, but we are given *peace,* God's wholeness and harmony, according to our work.

Shalom brings it all together: power, love, trust, and protection. *Shalom* makes our waiting fruitful. *Shalom* fills the silence with its melody of love. For God alone, for God's wholeness and perfect peace, our souls in silence wait. Amen.

Listening

❧

FOR PRAYER AND PONDERING

How does God speak to you? Might you have missed hearing God's voice because it came unexpectedly, in odd and "unspiritual" times and places?

Can you believe that power and love are compatible? Can you image a God who is simultaneously all-loving and all-powerful?

Our human loving is a pale reflection of God's love. Is there a place for power in your loving?

We are promised God's peace—*shalom*. What does this mean to you?

Endnotes

1. *St. Benedict's Rule for Monasteries,* trans. Leonard J. Doyle (Collegeville, Minn.: The Liturgical Press, 1948), 40.
2. Walter Brueggemann, *Praying the Psalms* (Winona, Minn.: St. Mary's Press, 1986), 16-17.
3. Ibid., 20.
4. William Blake, *Selected Poems* (London: Dent, 1982), 132.
5. In these days of heightened sensitivity to language, it is difficult to write about God without irritating or angering some readers. Pronouns are such difficult little words! Following the example of the psalmist, I have sometimes opted to use traditional language, but in full awareness that God is neither "he" nor "she"—but much, much

more. The God who made us, loves us, and keeps us cannot be reduced to a pronoun, either trendily correct or comfortably conservative.

6. "The kingdom of God is within you" is a variant reading.

7. Margaret Wise Brown, *The Runaway Bunny*, illustrations by Clement Hurd (New York: Harper, 1972).

8. Initials changed to protect the guilty or innocent, as the case may be.

Translations of Psalm 62

For God alone my soul in silence waits;
    from him comes my salvation.
He alone is my rock and my salvation,
    my stronghold, so that I shall not
        be greatly shaken.
How long will you assail me to crush me,
all of you together,
    as if you were a leaning fence,
        a toppling wall?
They seek only to bring me down from
my place of honor;
    lies are their chief delight.

Translations of Psalm 62

They bless with their lips,
    but in their hearts they curse.
For God alone my soul in silence waits;
    truly, my hope is in him.
He alone is my rock and my salvation,
    my stronghold, so that I shall not be shaken.
In God is my safety and my honor;

    God is my strong rock and my refuge.
Put your trust in him always, O people,
    pour out your hearts before him, for God
        is our refuge.
Those of high degree are but a fleeting breath,
    even those of low estate cannot be trusted.
On the scales they are lighter than a breath,
    all of them together.
Put no trust in extortion;
in robbery take no empty pride;
    though wealth increase, set not your heart upon it.
God has spoken once, twice have I heard it,
    that power belongs to God.
Steadfast love is yours, O Lord,
    for you repay everyone according
        to his deeds.

(The Book of Common Prayer 1979)

For God alone my soul waits in silence;
    from him comes my salvation.
He alone is my rock and my salvation,
    my fortress; I shall never be shaken.

How long will you assail a person,
    will you batter your victim, all of you,
    as you would a leaning wall,
        a tottering fence?
Their only plan is to bring down
        a person of prominence.
    They take pleasure in falsehood;
they bless with their mouths,
    but inwardly they curse.
For God alone my soul waits in silence,
    for my hope is from him.
He alone is my rock and my salvation,
    my fortress; I shall not be shaken.
On God rests my deliverance and my honor;
    my mighty rock, my refuge is in God.
Trust in him at all times, O people;
    pour out your heart before him;
    God is a refuge for us.
Those of low estate are but a breath,
    those of high estate are a delusion;
in the balances they go up;
    they are together lighter than a breath.
Put no confidence in extortion,

and set no vain hopes on robbery;
if riches increase, do not set
your heart on them.
Once God has spoken;
twice have I heard this:
that power belongs to God,
and steadfast love belongs to you, O Lord.
For you repay to all
according to their work.

(New Revised Standard Version)

135

In God alone there is rest for my soul,
   from him comes my safety;
he alone is my rock, my safety,
   my stronghold so that I stand unshaken.
How much longer will you set on a victim,
   all together, intent on murder,
like a rampart already leaning over,
   a wall already damaged?
Trickery is their only plan,
   deception their only pleasure,
with lies on their lips they pronounce a blessing,
   with a curse in their hearts.
Rest in God alone, my soul!
   He is the source of my hope.
He alone is my rock, my safety,
   my stronghold, so that I stand unwavering.
In God is my safety and my glory,
   the rock of my strength.
In God is my refuge; trust in him,
   you people, at all times.
Pour out your hearts to him,
   God is a refuge for us.
Ordinary people are a mere puff of wind,
   important people a delusion;
set both on the scales together,
   and they are lighter than a puff of wind.
Put no trust in extortion,

no empty hopes in robbery;
however much wealth may multiply,
    do not set your heart on it.
Once God has spoken,
    twice have I heard this:
Strength belongs to God,
    to you, Lord, faithful love;
    and you repay everyone as their deeds deserve.

(New Jerusalem Bible)

Truly my heart waits silently for God;
   my deliverance comes from him.
In truth he is my rock of deliverance,
   my tower of strength, so that I can
      stand unshaken.
   How long will you assail a man
     with your threats,
   all battering on a leaning wall?
In truth men plan to topple him from his height,
   and stamp on the fallen stones.
   With their lips they bless him, the hypocrites,
     but revile him in their hearts.
Truly my heart waits silently for God;
   ny hope of deliverance comes from him.
In truth he is my rock of deliverance,
   my tower of strength, so that I am unshaken.
   My deliverance and my honour depend upon God,
   God who is my rock of refuge and my shelter.
   Trust always in God, my people,
   pour out your hearts before him;
     God is our shelter.
   In very truth men are a puff of wind,
     all men are faithless;
   put them in the balance and they can only rise,
     all of them lighter than wind.
     Put no trust in extortion,
     do not be proud of stolen goods;

though wealth breeds wealth, set not
    your heart on it.
One thing God has spoken,
    two things I have learnt:
'Power belongs to God'
and 'True love, O Lord, is thine';
thou dost requite a man for his deeds.

(The New English Bible)

Cowley Publications is a ministry of the Society of St. John the Evangelist, a religious community for men in the Episcopal Church. Emerging from the Society's tradition of prayer, theological reflection, and diversity of mission, the press is centered in the rich heritage of the Anglican Communion.

Cowley Publications seeks to provide books, audio cassettes, and other resources for the ongoing theological exploration and spiritual development of the Episcopal Church and others in the body of Christ. To this end, it is dedicated to developing a new generation of theological writers, encouraging them to produce timely, creative, and stimulating publications of excellence, and making these publications available widely, reaching both clergy and lay persons.